The Art of Embroidery Design

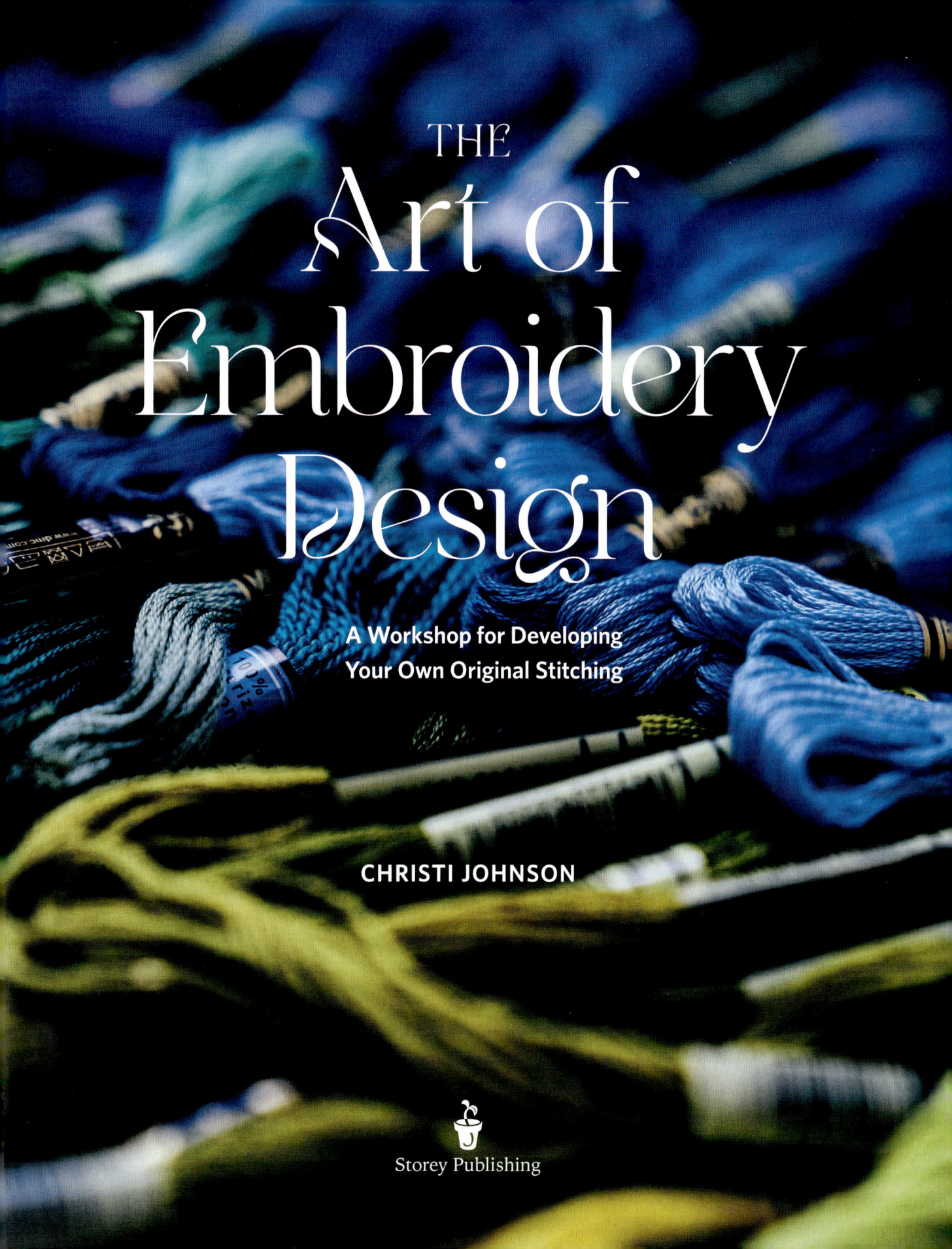

THE
Art of
Embroidery
Design

A Workshop for Developing
Your Own Original Stitching

CHRISTI JOHNSON

Storey Publishing

The mission of Storey Publishing is to serve our customers by
publishing practical information that encourages
personal independence in harmony with the environment.

Edited, art directed, and designed by Alethea Morrison

Cover photography by Mars Vilaubi © Storey Publishing, except author photo by © HeshPhoto, Inc.

Interior photography by © HeshPhoto, Inc., i–viii, 2, 4, 6, 7, 20, 56, 60, 61 snake shirt, 109, 120, 123, 126, 129 portrait, 134, 152, 187; Mars Vilaubi © Storey Publishing, 5, 9, 13, 14–16, 21–47, 55, 57, 61 background, 64–71, 73–77, 80, 81, 85–91, 94–97, 99, 100, 104–108, 110–115, 118, 119, 121, 127, 129 symbol, 133, 135, 137, 139, 140 b., 141, 143–151, 154, 159–163, 186

Additional photography by © Alina Stoenescu/ Shutterstock, 17 t.; Anna Hultin, 116 b., 117; Beth Hoyes, 101–103; Brooke Forwood, 116 t.; Ciara LeRoy, 140 t.; © Christi Johnson, 10, 59; Courtesy of Elizabeth Pawle, 62, 63; Elizabeth Sanders, 92 t.; Gabriela Martínez Ortiz by Daniela Constantini, 79; Gabriela Martínez Ortiz by Ofelia & Antelmo, 78; © Heritage Image Partnership Ltd/Alamy Stock Photo, 12; © Joshua Small-Photographer/Shutterstock, 17 m.; © Linda Hughes Photography/Shutterstock, 17 b.; Lindzeanne, 82, 83; Installation view of the exhibition Pacita Abad: A Million Things to Say at the Museum of Contemporary Art and Design (MCAD), Manila, 12 April–1 July 2018. Photo by At Maculangan/Pioneer Studios for MCAD, Manila. © MCAD, Manila, 98; © mauritius images GmbH/ Alamy Stock Photo, 52; © Nancy J. Ondra/Shutterstock, 84 t.; From the collections of the Philadelphia Museum of Art, 51; © propclothsamplers, 70 b.l. & t.; © Sarah K. Benning, 92 b.l. & b.r., 93; © Susan Montgomery/ Shutterstock, 84 b.; © Suzuki Kaku/Alamy Stock Photo, 48, 49; © Tawna Brown/Alamy Stock Photo, 53; Tessa Perlow, 124, 125; Valeria Duque Posada, 130, 131; © Werner Forman/Getty Images, 50

Illustrations by © Nina Chakrabarti, except © Christi Johnson, 54, 72, 84, 132

Text © 2025 by Christi Johnson

Storey books may be purchased in bulk for business, educational, or promotional use. Special editions or book excerpts can also be created to specification. For details, please contact your local bookseller or the Hachette Book Group Special Markets Department at special.markets@hbgusa.com.

Storey Publishing
210 MASS MoCA Way
North Adams, MA 01247
storey.com

Storey Publishing is an imprint of Workman Publishing, a division of Hachette Book Group, Inc., 1290 Avenue of the Americas, New York, NY 10104. The Storey Publishing name and logo are registered trademarks of Hachette Book Group, Inc.

ISBNs: 978-1-63586-766-4 (hardcover); 978-1-63586-814-2 (fixed format EPUB); 978-1-63586-936-1 (fixed format PDF); 978-1-63586-937-8 (fixed format Kindle)

Printed in China through Asia Pacific Offset on paper from responsible sources
10 9 8 7 6 5 4 3 2 1

Library of Congress Cataloging-in-Publication Data on file

To my little one

Contents

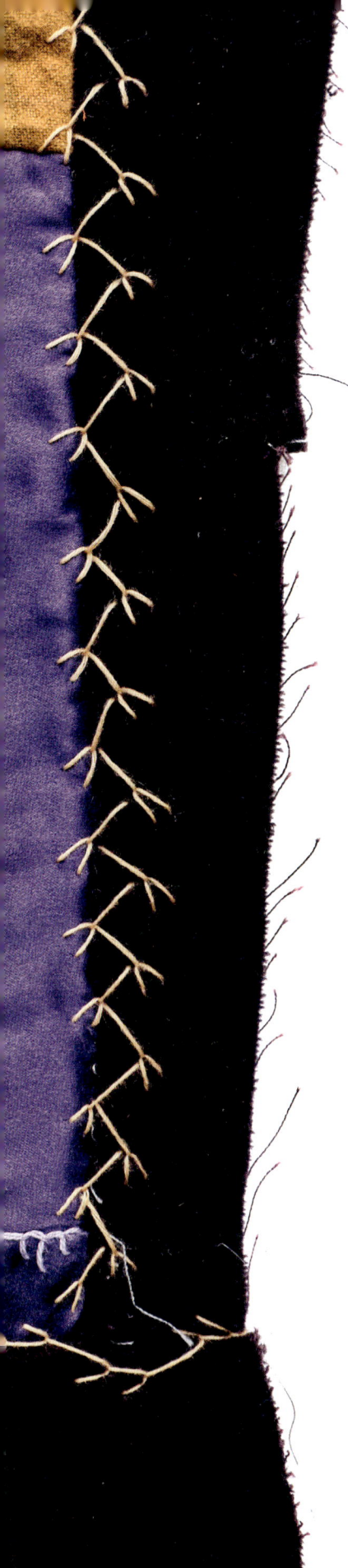

An Invitation
TO PERSONAL EXPRESSION

Stitching runs in my blood, and yours, too. If you go back even just a couple of generations, most likely there were works of art in your family that have since perished alongside their creators. Quiet expressions made in rare moments of solitude, learned from the hands of their elders, passed down to the hands of their children. I wrote this book for anyone who wishes someone had taught them this skill, and especially for those of you who may have already learned but were reprimanded for not having done it the "right way."

I grew up in a pile of fabric scraps, stitching my way through life, but it wasn't until my late twenties that I discovered my path to unique personal expression through the art of embroidery. As I dove headfirst into learning as much as I could about each stitch, I became eager to pull others into the experience—not just of stitching, but the creative act itself.

Teaching embroidery is fun for me, but what really lights me up is working through creative blocks. From perfectionism to fear of the blank page, these blocks only serve to hinder our growth and ability to clearly express ourselves. I see creativity as an opportunity for liberation and a chance to explore new ways of thinking and being.

Embroidery is an ideal entry into a creative practice: The process is as simple or as complex as you'd like, and it always guides you slowly from an idea in your head to art you can hold in your hands. Most of my first embroideries—wait, nearly *all* of my embroideries—have misplaced threads, drooping letters, and crooked lines with a mind all their own. These threads reflect the imperfect nature of my own existence but, more so than any other art form, seem to do so beautifully in a way that is much easier to accept . . . and maybe even forgive.

This is a book for anyone with a desire to speak through images. Even if you don't consider yourself creative, I hope to help you find your own language of expression.

You Are Enough

Being fortunate enough to have my artistic tendencies nurtured from an early age, I once thought that my talents were a divine gift, that I was special. Throughout my experience studying art and design, and then teaching various textile arts, I learned that creativity is in fact available to everyone.

Sure, some people are more naturally inclined toward the arts, but even those who "can't draw a straight line" seem able to discover a well of potential with enough focused practice. Some of the less artistic students I went to school with—who committed time and effort to developing their creative expression—proved to me that creativity is a skill we can learn, not just a talent we are blessed with.

This book is all about developing that skill. We focus on how to do this through the art of embroidery, in the format of a workshop.

This is not a book of patterns to be replicated. This is a book that invites you to be a part of the process of image creation.

Welcome to My Workshop

Throughout these pages are sections called Sketchbook Experiment and Sampler Development, where I offer hands-on exercises that encourage an exploration of materials and concepts. My hope is that when you engage with these exercises, you'll strengthen and activate your creative muscles for expression. And if those muscles still feel stiff, I offer gentle guidance on how to loosen up in sections called Overcoming Resistance. I invite you to take this workshop in whatever way suits you—from beginning to end, as it was built, taking a week or so to practice each included experiment—or jump around and have fun at any pace.

* **Chapter 1.** We begin by starting a creative habit. All you'll need is a notebook and a few supplies for stitching, so you can collect imagery and practice making marks on fabric.

* **Chapter 2.** We look at embroidery from around the world and observe many different styles and methods of personalizing cloth with stitches.

* **Chapter 3.** I teach you about design, untangling and explaining the principles of line, texture, color, and composition, so you have the confidence to create your own images in thread, even if you can't draw (see page 61)!

* **Chapter 4.** We learn how inspiration works with design to create a cohesive vision.

* **Chapter 5.** We tie all this together and you'll apply what you've learned to a work of art.

If you are new to embroidery, the appendix Embroidery Basics (see page 154) will set you up with some fundamental skills. The final appendix, Stitch Methods (see page 159), has detailed step-by-step, illustrated instructions for all of the common embroidery stitches as well as many less common ones, for those of you interested in expanding your techniques for interesting effects.

Throughout, I'll share work from my own creative process and work from embroidery artists I admire, so you can study how other people have created unique designs.

1
Practicing Creativity

TOOLS FOR DEVELOPING YOUR UNIQUE ARTISTIC VOICE

In this section of the workshop, you'll introduce a creative practice (artistic habit, craft ritual, getting into the groove, whatever you want to call it) to your schedule, which not only helps you expand your practical skills but also supports creativity in other areas of your life. Whether you're innately driven to create, or don't consider yourself creative but always find yourself seeing handmade items and thinking "Wow, I really wish I could do that," you will benefit immensely from developing a creative practice.

My Creative Process

How we develop artwork looks completely different for every individual, and I by no means want to prescribe a process that is, at its heart, intuitive. But I'm always interested to hear from other artists and makers about their process and glean new methods to introduce into my own work, so I'll share what I do.

How I Find Inspiration

The permanence of markers and pens helps release me from the pursuit of perfection and allows me to express myself more freely.

My sketchbook serves as a depository of imagery—things I see throughout my day, little details I notice, or compositional arrangements that strike me. I try to work in a bold pen on occasion; it forces me to make confident marks that I can't redo. If I'm feeling restless, I'll often pull out a pile of markers and let them swirl and scribble across the page without rhyme or reason.

I also devour richly illustrated books to find inspiration outside of stitching. From mythology and archaeology to botanical drawings and ancient architecture, I allow myself to be drawn to a book (or three), pull them out, and sketch the details that draw me in.

During the times I'm devoting myself to absorbing inspiration, I allow stillness, meditation, and other forms of quieting the mind to be a part of my practice—closing my eyes, seeing what comes up, accepting and embracing any weirdness that might arise.

How I Plan a Design

Once I have an idea for what I want my next work to be about, I refer to my sketchbook and pull out the elements that seem most relevant. I'll sketch these together on a page and begin to visualize how they might combine. I begin to balance areas of outline, fill, and texture; I gather thread colors that might support my idea and the images I've chosen.

In developing sketches for this embroidered neckline, I started with a basic layout in pencil, then detailed the colors and direction of stitches with a bold marker.

I don't try to force a concept intellectually. I let intuition and conscious reason balance each other. Sometimes I don't know why I'm adding something until the work is done! Reducing immediate judgment of my work and resisting the urge to overanalyze each element allows me to be a clear channel for unexpected inspiration.

Over many years, I've learned to accept that sometimes things don't work out as planned (or at all, really). And that lesson is an incredibly important part of the work. I have a pile of failed attempts, and I love being able to dig back through them and find the absolute perfect placement or purpose for the piece that I tossed aside many months, or even years, ago. The benefit of tolerating failure is that there is more room for experimentation, allowing materials and concepts to take shape without forcing an idea upon them.

You may find that your own creative process looks entirely different, and that's okay! However you work, let's get our tools together and begin.

Your Tool Kit

Throughout this book, we're going to dive into each aspect of design through both *sketching* and *stitching*. When we spend time with these teachings, practicing them with our mind and our hands, we begin to record these techniques into muscle memory.

Through approaching the exercises of this workshop with curiosity and an openness to discovery, we allow room to make mistakes. We learn more about how these elements of design work with one another. Getting outside our heads and experimenting with materials in real life also allows new ideas to blossom. Each past creation helps support potential future creations.

> Once we memorize design techniques, we cross the threshold from practice to meaningful personal expression.

By knowing these techniques deeply, we can express meaning through them. Think about the written page as an example: a collection of 26 symbols composing words that we know the meaning of without second thought. Similarly, a fluency with design methods allows us to express ourselves easily in the medium of embroidery.

The Sketchbook

If you're anything like me, you may think that a sketchbook should be a meticulous collection of amazing drawings and well-worded thoughts, but then . . . when you try to keep your own sketchbook, you start feeling like maybe it's not good enough, or like you shouldn't be wasting paper with these scribbles and noncohesive thoughts. I urge you to reconsider. My sketchbooks are full of notes I don't need, sketches I don't like, and illegible, random thoughts. However, the process of keeping all these sketches and notes in the same place begins to show its worth over time. You look at a sketch from last month, in conjunction with a thought you had last week, and realize the infinite potential available when you start stringing together these ideas.

So how do we *use* our sketchbook? Where do we find all the information to collect here? If we bring it with us everywhere, we'll find plenty of inspiration. So, here's my challenge to you: Each day for the next seven days, find at least five visually inspiring moments and capture them in your book.

Go beyond what you see on social media or the internet. From the subtle texture in the petals of a flower to the bold graphics on a bottle of seltzer, start to see everything you interact with in everyday life as an opportunity for design. On page 17, I include prompts for exploring the world around you, so no excuses about not knowing what to draw! Remember, the goal is to develop your very own style, so allow yourself to be free with these choices, and keep it sketchy. There is no pressure.

Finding your own style is the sort of process that lasts a lifetime, but it starts by becoming aware of what lights you up.

As you start, you may not find focus, and that's okay. If your drawings seem to be random and have no relation, you'll know you're in the stage of keeping yourself open to all possibilities; you can edit later.

So go ahead, choose a sketchbook, or reassign a journal as the place you'll collect images for the remainder of this workshop. Sketch them throughout the day or capture moments with your camera and then translate them into sketches at the end of the day. Whatever works for you is fine; just be sure you're keeping your eyes wide open for beauty and inspiration wherever you go.

CHOOSING A SKETCHBOOK

As far as notebooks go, there are three obvious choices: lined pages, blank pages, and grid pages—either a dot grid or an actual grid. Of these, I prefer either dot grid or blank pages. While grids and lines are nice, they tend to obstruct the drawings, especially if you use pencil. Dot grids allow you to use the pages for both writing and drawing, without getting in the way. There is also the size of the notebook to consider. Whatever is convenient for you is best, but I *love* the half-letter size, as it fits easily in a bag for travel.

The Sampler

The process of developing a new skill might feel overwhelming, or like you want to start all the things at once, so I recommend beginning with a sampler. Samplers are the traditional method of learning embroidery, but let's make them less about seeking perfection and more about design exploration. Collecting our experiments in one place, we'll create a reference guide for when we're stuck. This collection of stitches isn't meant to be a showstopper museum piece but rather a tool for informing later artwork. Writing or even embroidering the names of each stitch helps the future functionality of the sampler.

Don't get caught up in overplanning your sampler. Remember that the goal is to create a future reference guide and learn about composition, color choices, and time management along the way. For example, as you practice an intricate blanket stitch variation on your sampler, you'll find out how long the stitch takes and maybe decide to reserve that time-consuming option for accents instead of the bulk of a design.

SOME IDEAS FOR SAMPLERS

* Create a sampler book with pages and covers. (See Sampler Book on page 18 for directions.)
* Plan a small quilt, pillow, or wall piece with sections marked off for each stitch. (See Sampler Grid on page 19.)
* More of a freestyle maker? Designate a large piece of fabric as your "stitch sketchbook" and allow the stitches to meander across the fabric freely. (See Freestyle Sampler on page 19.)

Needlework samplers such as this seventeenth-century English example at left were historically demonstrations of skill and achievement.

A contemporary approach to samplers focuses on exploration and experimentation rather than perfection. Some of my students have shared their work.

▶ Amy Freyn practiced stitches on separate cloth squares that she bound into a book.

▶▶ Gretchen Thayer chose a freestyle approach, with different stitch experiments meandering across a single piece of fabric.

▼ Kirstin Pinit created a grid of triangles for her experiments.

GATHERING SUPPLIES

We often think we need to buy all sorts of supplies to get going on a new project, but the beauty of embroidery is that it requires so *little* to get started and can be done practically anywhere, with just about anything.

Fabric

Woven fabrics, rather than stretchy knits like T-shirt material, work best for embroidery. For beginners, I don't recommend lightweight fabrics that you can see through or fabrics too dense to pass a needle through without forcing. Sturdy woven cloth like muslin, broadcloth, and most linens hold the tension of the threads without bunching. The best test for whether a particular fabric works well for embroidery is to make a few sample stitches somewhere inconspicuous.

You don't necessarily need to buy new. Is there scrap fabric available? Maybe something in your closet is too ripped or stained to give away. Can you cut out usable parts of the fabric to embroider on?

Threads

I mostly use six-ply embroidery floss, which is common, easy to find, and inexpensive. DMC is my brand of choice thanks to the wide range of colors and high quality. Because the floss is composed of six strands, you can split it, so you essentially have six sizes of thread in one convenient package! However, if you can fit a strand of fiber through the eye of a needle, and it doesn't break when you're stitching, you can use it as an embroidery thread.

Needles

I recommend chenille and tapestry needles. They have large eyes, making them easy to thread, and come in many sizes. Chenille needles have a sharp point that works great on most fabrics, while tapestry needles have a dull tip that works best on fabrics with a thick, open weave, such as heavy linens and handwoven cloth. For directions on how to thread a needle, see page 155.

- **FOR GENERAL USE:** I use a size 24 needle for three to six strands of embroidery floss on most medium-weight fabrics.

- **FOR THICKER THREADS AND FABRICS:** If I'm using all six strands of embroidery floss or wool tapestry yarns on a heavier fabric, I use size 22.

- **FOR THINNER THREADS AND FABRICS:** If I'm using fewer than three strands of embroidery floss or fine silk threads, I use size 26. Thin fabrics such as cotton poplin also require a finer needle, so you don't make large holes in delicate cloth. Embroidery needles tend to have smaller eyes than chenille needles, but they are a good option for thinner threads, fine details, and delicate fabrics.

Embroidery Hoop

Embroidery hoops are especially helpful for beginners and when using lighter-weight fabrics. I prefer hoops made of wood or bamboo. A hoop holds the fabric taut, so you are less likely to pull the stitches too tight, which causes puckering and bunching. For heavy fabrics like denim and canvas, using the hoop might not be possible, so just be sure you aren't pulling your stitches too tight. For directions on how to set up your hoop, see page 156.

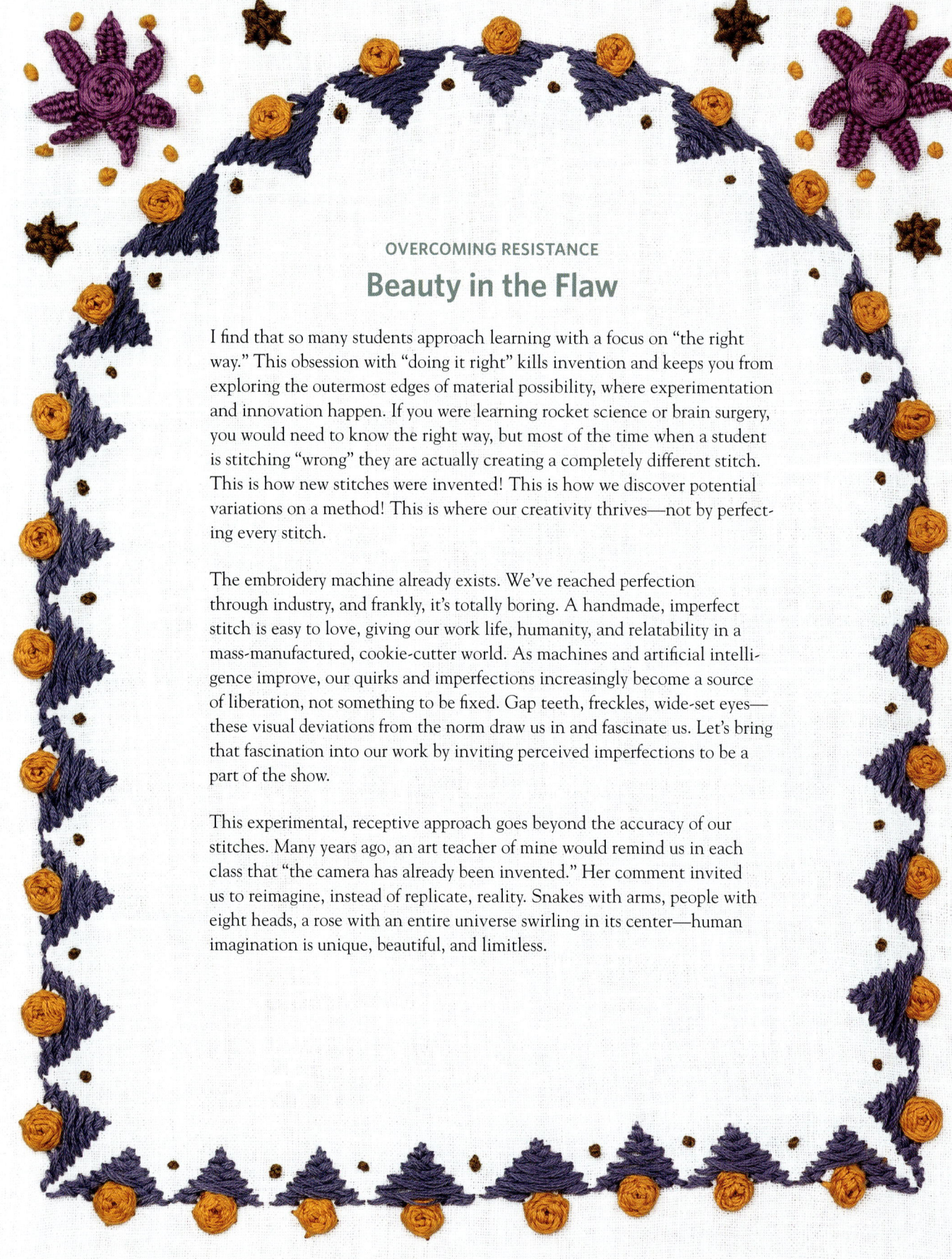

Beauty in the Flaw

I find that so many students approach learning with a focus on "the right way." This obsession with "doing it right" kills invention and keeps you from exploring the outermost edges of material possibility, where experimentation and innovation happen. If you were learning rocket science or brain surgery, you would need to know the right way, but most of the time when a student is stitching "wrong" they are actually creating a completely different stitch. This is how new stitches were invented! This is how we discover potential variations on a method! This is where our creativity thrives—not by perfecting every stitch.

The embroidery machine already exists. We've reached perfection through industry, and frankly, it's totally boring. A handmade, imperfect stitch is easy to love, giving our work life, humanity, and relatability in a mass-manufactured, cookie-cutter world. As machines and artificial intelligence improve, our quirks and imperfections increasingly become a source of liberation, not something to be fixed. Gap teeth, freckles, wide-set eyes—these visual deviations from the norm draw us in and fascinate us. Let's bring that fascination into our work by inviting perceived imperfections to be a part of the show.

This experimental, receptive approach goes beyond the accuracy of our stitches. Many years ago, an art teacher of mine would remind us in each class that "the camera has already been invented." Her comment invited us to reimagine, instead of replicate, reality. Snakes with arms, people with eight heads, a rose with an entire universe swirling in its center—human imagination is unique, beautiful, and limitless.

Observing What's Around You

Fill one entire page for each of the following prompts (three pages total):

* Using your sketchbook, take note of architectural details in your home, neighborhood, or city. Allow these details to help you develop patterns and repetitions of geometric forms. Even the most mundane suburban shopping plaza might hide in plain view undulations of pillars, moldings, fences, and sewer grates from which to draw inspiration.

* Choose two or three plants to focus intently on, whether you find them in a house or building, a garden, or an entire forest. In what ways do their elements repeat—or not? What basic shapes compose their parts? How would you attempt to describe their textures using lines?

* Look at your wardrobe, your home decor, and even your "most wanted" shopping list. What textures commonly repeat? When looking at the fabric prints in your life, what shapes make up these prints?

Creating the Surface

Set up your sampler so you're prepared for the rest of the workshop. There are many ways to create a sampler book, but here is an option that gives clean finished edges and hides the messy backside of your stitches. There will be 12 prompts for stitching in your sampler. You might allow two or three extra spaces if you'd like to test texture and color combinations for your final project in the last chapter. This makes a total of 12 to 15 positions to prepare for your sampler, and 2" or less should be enough space for each. Here are a few formats to choose from.

Sampler Book

Your finished sampler will be a 5" × 7" book made of six pages, plus a front cover and back cover. Each page and cover is a 10" × 7" rectangle "sheet" folded in half. The raw edges become the spine of the book, while the fold becomes the edge of the page. The backs of your stitches will hide inside the middle of each folded sheet.

1. Cut a 10" × 35" piece of fabric. Using an erasable fabric marker (see page 157 for more on marking tools), draw a line down the middle of the length of the fabric and at 7" increments across the width. The blue lines in the diagram at right indicate where to mark.

2. Each 5" × 7" rectangle on your fabric is one page of your sampler or a cover. Each page will accommodate two sampler experiments. Don't stitch edge to edge. Focus your designs instead on the center of the page and allow blank space around the edges. These are known as margins in bookmaking. If you're feeling super precise, mark two 2" squares on each page as shown in the diagram.

3. Use a 6" hoop to work on your sampler as you progress through the Sampler Development experiments throughout the book. Assemble your sampler book *after* you finish stitching.

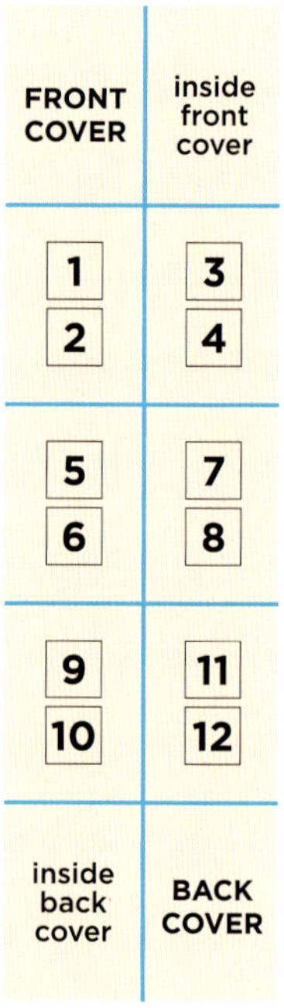

FRONT COVER	inside front cover
1 2	3 4
5 6	7 8
9 10	11 12
inside back cover	BACK COVER

Steps 1 and 2

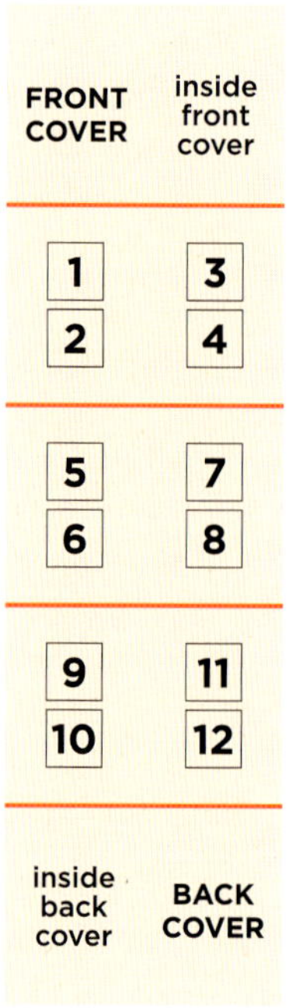

FRONT COVER	inside front cover
1 2	3 4
5 6	7 8
9 10	11 12
inside back cover	BACK COVER

Step 4

4. After you've completed a stitched sampler, cut *only* on the lines marked along the 10" width. The cut lines are indicated in red in the diagram above.

5. Fold each sheet in half along the fold line, right sides facing. (You should be seeing the back of the stitching on both sides.) Stitch the top and bottom edges together ½" from each edge

using a running stitch (see page 165) or sewing machine.

6. Turn the fabric right side out to hide the sewn edges and backsides of the embroidery.

7. When you've finished all the pages and covers, stack them so that the raw edges are aligned. Use a sewing machine with a heavy-duty needle or hand-sew using the blanket stitch (see page 178) to assemble the book. With 10 layers of fabric, your book will be thick, and you may need to use an awl or a push pin to create holes within which to stitch.

8. If you want to hide the raw edges of the spine, use a 1½" × 7" strip of felt wrapped around the spine and secured with fabric glue.

Variation

If you want to be able to peek at the backsides of your embroidered pages for later reference rather than hiding them permanently, follow steps 1 through 4. Then fold the top and bottom edges of each sheet ½" to the back. Iron in place and stitch to secure using a simple running stitch, a sewing machine, or even a different decorative stitch for each sheet. Fold each sheet in half, back sides facing. (You should be seeing the front of the stitching on both sides.) Follow steps 7 and 8.

Sampler Grid

You may want your sampler experiments to embellish a piece of fabric for a small quilt, pillow sham, or wall piece. To keep the pressure off, plan the sampler as an addition to your creative space, not as a formal piece of decor. Start with a piece of fabric at least 12" × 14", and mark 12 to 15 separate areas for each experiment. Leave at least 3" of space on each outer edge of the cloth so that you can not only work with the fabric in an embroidery hoop but also leave room for a finishing hem later if desired. The sampler positions might be composed of squares, circles, even triangles! For making neat circles, trace a 2" jar lid.

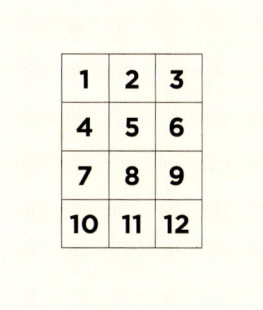

Freestyle Sampler

Feel free to practice without an organized plan, stitching each sampler exercise wherever it feels right in the moment. Starting with a large piece of fabric at least 12" × 14", mark a line 3" from each edge. (See page 157 for tips on marking tools.) Try to keep your stitches within the inner 6" × 8" frame so that you can not only work with the fabric in an embroidery hoop but also leave room for a finishing hem later if desired.

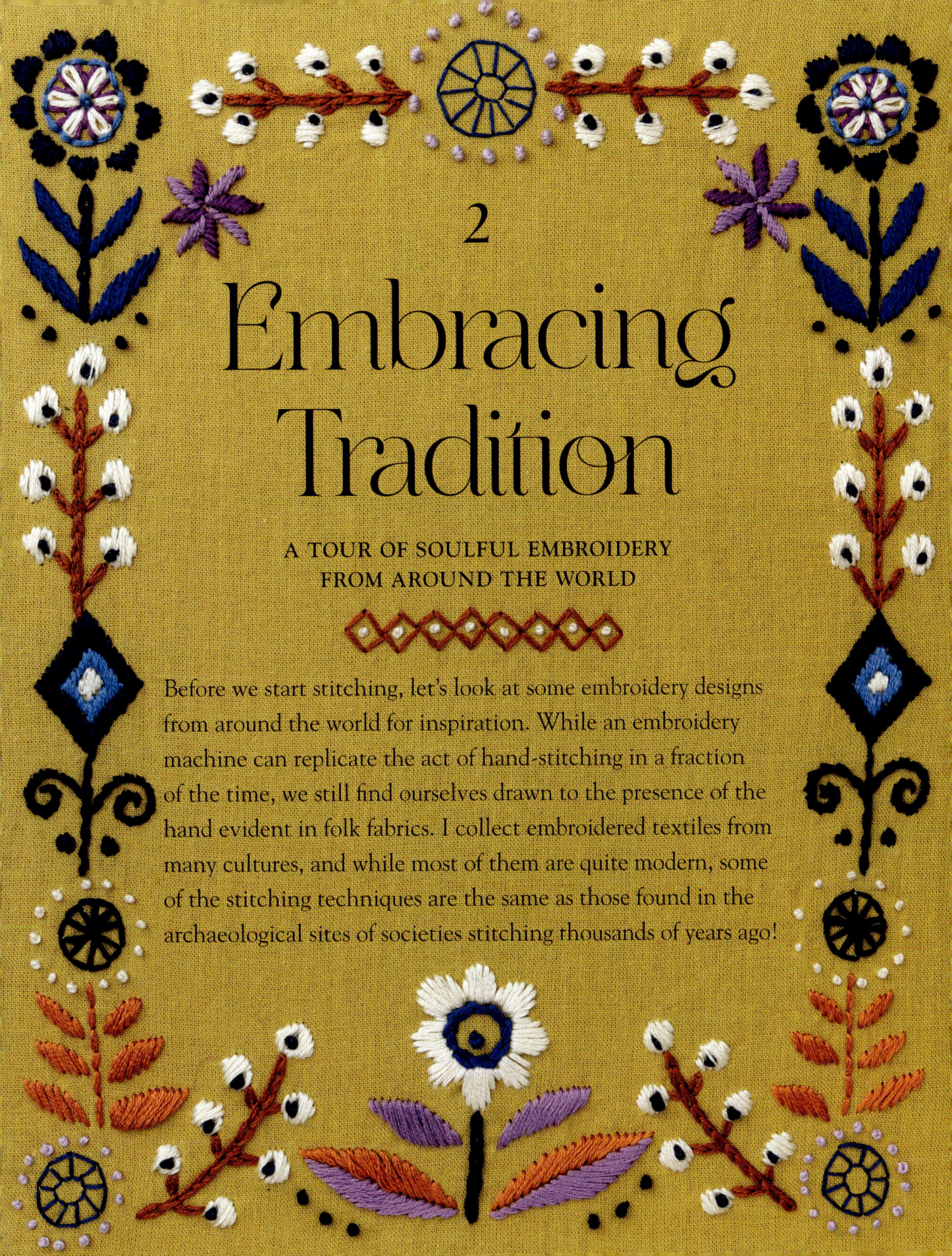

2

Embracing Tradition

A TOUR OF SOULFUL EMBROIDERY FROM AROUND THE WORLD

Before we start stitching, let's look at some embroidery designs from around the world for inspiration. While an embroidery machine can replicate the act of hand-stitching in a fraction of the time, we still find ourselves drawn to the presence of the hand evident in folk fabrics. I collect embroidered textiles from many cultures, and while most of them are quite modern, some of the stitching techniques are the same as those found in the archaeological sites of societies stitching thousands of years ago!

Stitching Stories

Textiles are, from their earliest creation, a medium for storytelling. Fundamentally, *text* and *textile* emerge from the same source—the Latin word *texere*, meaning "to weave." We weave worlds through the stringing of words. Countless mythologies from around the globe, including Greek and Dogon, describe the origin of human existence through textile terminology.

Textiles have supported the evolution of human community in many ways. We are more mobile when we can strap babies to our backs. Collecting food in lightweight containers, such as sewn animal hides, allows us to be more efficient during harvest. The insulating yet breathable warmth that clothing provides gives us a much wider range of places to live.

Shortly after lashing together hides or cloth, we discovered that we could mark fabric symbolically to support our hopes and goals. We stitched protective charms on the wrappings of a newborn baby; symbols of fertility and abundance on the skirts of those wishing to bear children; the desire for bravery on cloth worn by those heading out for a hunt.

Historically, many folk embroideries are stitched around the neck, the sleeve openings, the seams, and across the chest and the pelvic region. Such stitching invites protection, a way to confuse evil spirits so they will not enter through our clothes. Embroidering with alternating contrast colors or spiraling patterns, even adding sparkling sequins or mirrors, all began as a form of protection via distraction. Embroidered hats, headdresses, and other head coverings were a way to protect a crucial part of our bodies while also appealing to divinities who may be glancing down our way.

Many cultures embellish fabrics to mark rites of passage. Cloth adornments for marriage and death ceremonies often display a lifetime of stitches, not only because it looks good but also because threads are a medium for holding some of our deepest beliefs.

See Stitch Methods (starting on page 159) for instruction on all the stitches mentioned in this chapter.

▶**Front:** An embroidery from Mexico, stitched in thick wool yarns using a closed herringbone stitch. The mix of neutrals and neons in a full-coverage design makes for a vibrant, exciting work of art.

▲**Back:** When you look at the backside of the cloth, you can see how the herringbone stitch leaves most of the thread on the front of the fabric, creating a delicate outline on the back and conserving materials.

◄**Front:** A bouquet of bright flowers on handwoven cloth from Guatemala. An artist has created this design using the satin stitch, which gives a more raised effect. Satin stitch tends to "puff" up, especially in this hearty wool yarn.

▼**Back:** With satin stitch, the backside of the cloth looks nearly the same as the front.

Front: A radial design from India (said to be from the Kutch region of Gujarat), where each edge of the border acts as its own horizon line. No matter which way you turn the cloth, animals are right side up along the bottom edge.

Detail: The artist created this piece with a mix of Bokhara couching stitches (for the filled-in areas) and running stitch (for the border). Running stitch in a very thin white yarn covers the background, giving a subtle overall texture.

◄ The long running stitches in the border, with just a small amount of space between each stitch, allows the white of the fabric to create a diamond pattern.

▲**Front:** In a process called appliqué, a Peruvian artist patched separate pieces of fabric in different colors on top of the main fabric surface. Some pieces have stuffing underneath to create even more dimension. Dozens of different stitches embellish the scene: straight stitch, satin stitch, blanket stitch, stem stitch, herringbone stitch, and detached chain stitch, just to name a few.

▶**Detail:** The variations in thread types add another layer of dimension—from thick wool strands to single cotton threads. In a marvelous stroke of creativity, the artist gave some of the farmers tiny shovels made of real wood!

▶ Front: This traditional Panamanian Mola cloth is mostly appliqué.

▼ Detail: Note the special attention shown on the face, embroidered with incredibly tiny chain stitches using a single strand of thread.

◄Front: This stunner came from the Hmong hill tribe located in Thailand. Using satin stitching with an interesting method of long and short stitches, the artist added French knots in highly contrasting colors to create this mesmerizing design.

►Detail: In keeping with the style of most modern Hmong embroideries, the edges are bordered with ribbons sewn on by machine, and the bottom has a heavy beaded fringe for maximum coverage and decoration.

▼**Front:** The Banjara, a nomadic group from India, embroider elaborate necklines. This simpler design is made up entirely of chain stitch.

▶**Detail:** Showing both the front and backside of the cloth

▼**Front:** This more complex version of a Banjara neckline includes shisha mirrors, couched threads, and a wide variety of stitches from satin stitch to detached chain stitches.

▶**Detail:** Showing the front at top and the back at bottom

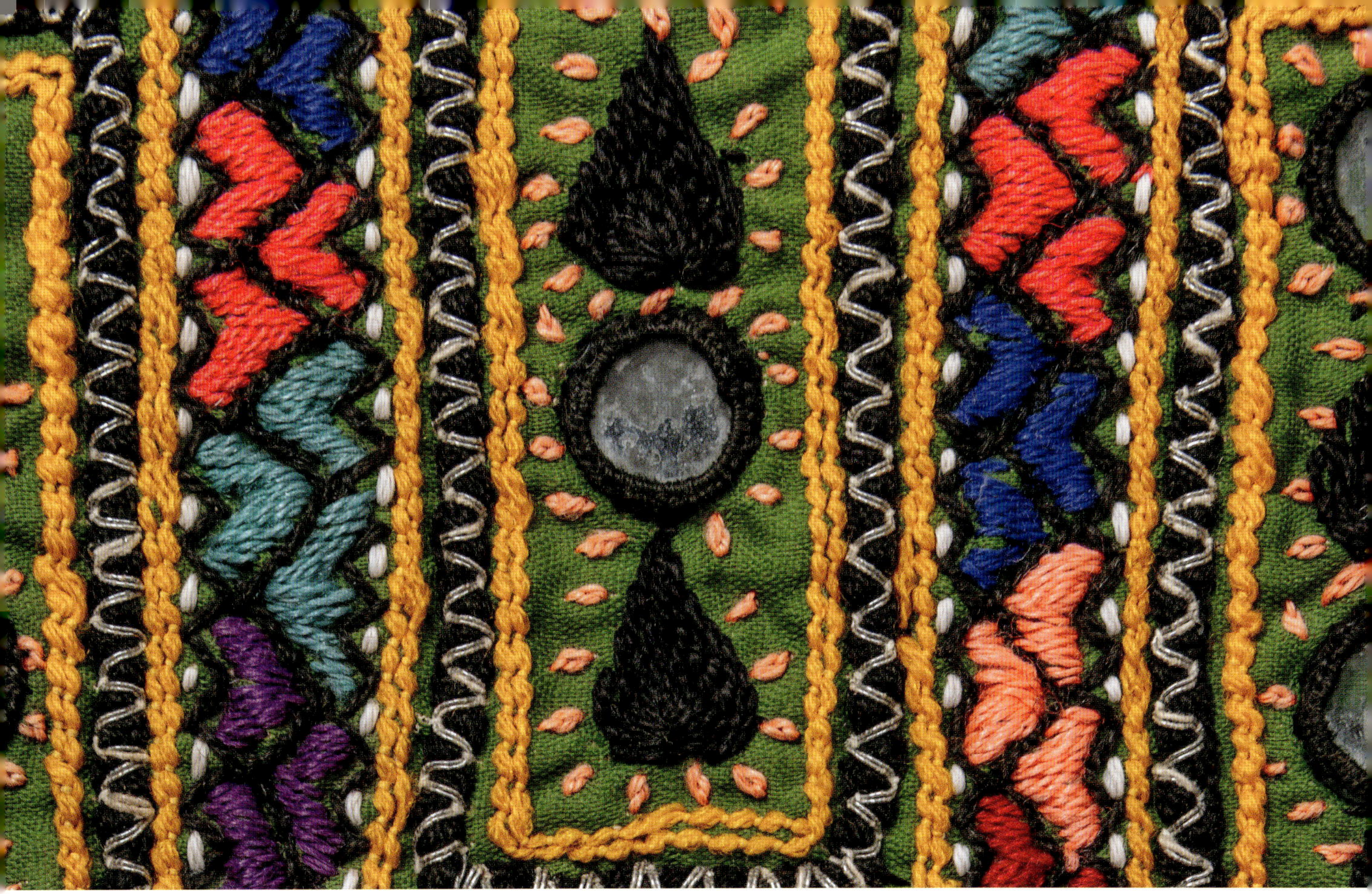
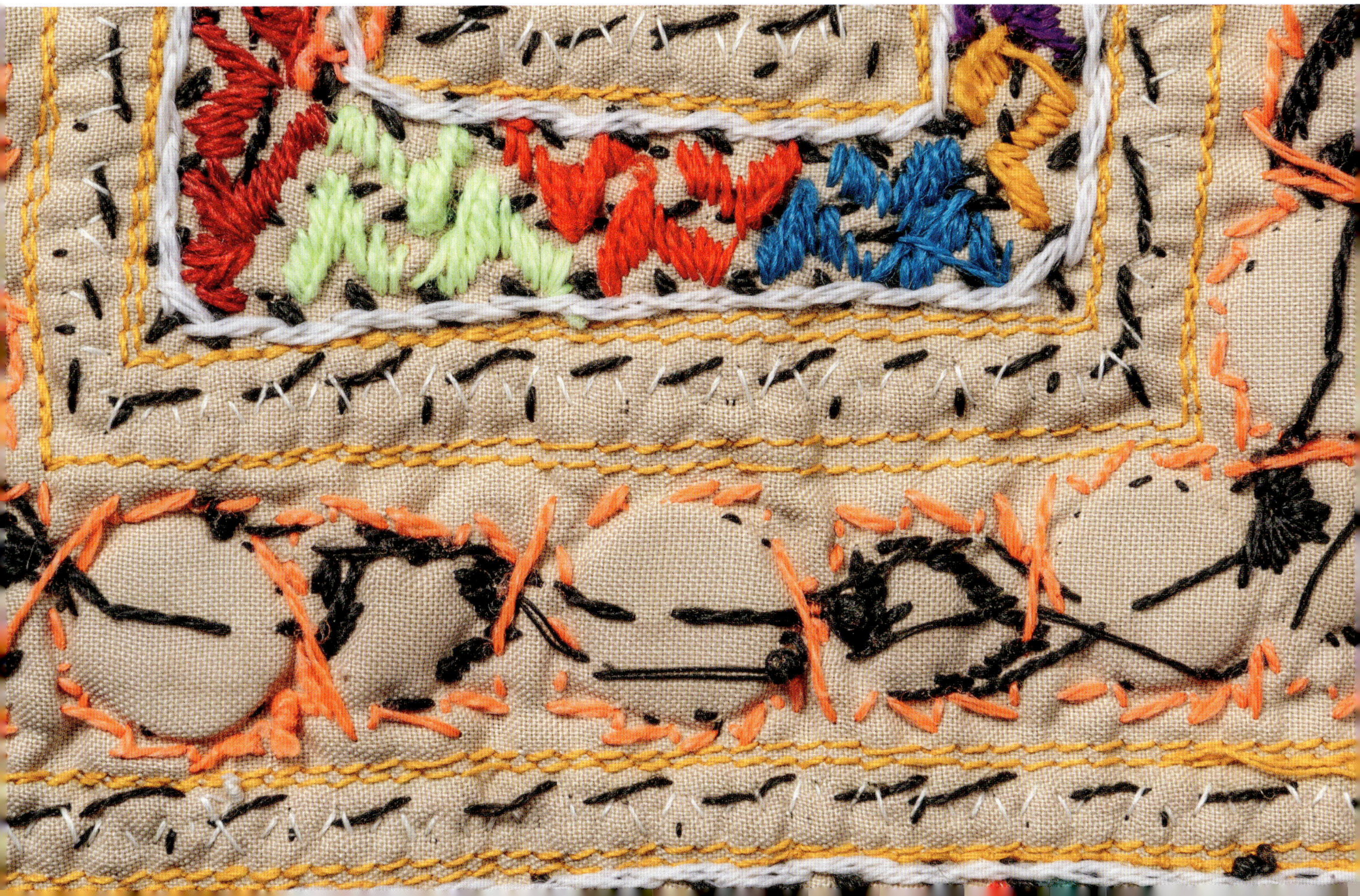

▼**Front:** Judging from the amount of sewing around the edges of these Banjara necklines, they were removed from their original garment and attached to a new garment several times.

▶Detail

▼**Front:** The Uzbek people create embroidered pieces called suzani, often as part of a wedding dowry. Suzani are used in many ways, from bedspreads to wrapping items for storage.

▶**Detail:** Suzani are usually composed almost entirely of Bokhara or Roumanian couching stitches in cotton threads, creating a textural surface that seems nearly woven into the base fabric.

▲**Back:** The back shows the original colors of the fabric and threads, which have faded significantly.

▲**Front:** Tenango is a traditional style of embroidery from the Hidalgo region of Mexico. The Indigenous Otomí-Tepehua people use a closed herringbone stitch.

◄**Back:** Much like the other Mexican embroidery shown, just the outline of the design is visible on the reverse of the fabric. What makes Tenango special is the way knots are created on the surface of the fabric; the tails of the knots are hidden underneath the thick stitches, which cleans up the backside of the work.

▶**Detail**

◄**Front:** This tunic, said to be from West Bengal, has been worked in a style of embroidery known as Kantha.

Detail: The artist used running stitch patterns as both outline and fill for this design. By laying the running stitch in a "brick" pattern, with alternating stitches coming to the surface, areas appear evenly filled. When the same running stitch pattern is repeated side by side, it creates a striped appearance.

◂**Front:** A Chinese embroidery depicts bamboo, peonies, and a peacock.

▸**Detail:** Created mostly with satin stitch using very fine silk threads, the effect is incredibly smooth, allowing the straight stitches that illustrate the feathers of the peacock to stand out.

Front: An embroidery from the Paracas culture of Peru

Detail: Though they appear almost woven into the fabric, these characters are actually created with rows upon rows of delicate stem stitches.

▲ Embroidered mostly with cotton on imported cloth, this type of elaborate robe was worn by royal women at the Bornu court in northeastern Nigeria.

▶ Working with scrap threads from unraveled garments, African American folk artist Charlie Logan (1893–1984) created his own personal costume of layered fabrics and found objects, which also included a cane, bag, and hat entirely covered in embellishment.

Inspiration, Not Imitation

The purpose of sharing existing art is not for you to imitate it, but to explore design through the lens of other cultures and individuals. Studying embroidery created outside of our own heritage helps emphasize the message that creativity and art belong to all of us. Art education in the modern era often focuses on realism, perspective, and the replication of real life. Studying folk art from around the world and across time stimulates our imagination to run free, demonstrating an approach to imagery that is often very personal and does not require a degree in life drawing to achieve.

I enjoy seeing how another artist stitched and styled their work in a way I couldn't imagine. I then combine what I learn with my own style, so that I'm contributing to the evolution of our collective designs, instead of just adding to the sea of imitations. That said, if someone provides you with patterns, copy away! Patterns are great and I love them. But also know that you have the fundamental human ability to develop your own vision and communicate it with needle and thread.

An Indigenous Tzotzil Maya woman stitching traditional Zinacantán embroidery in Chiapas, Mexico

A tanned moosehide jacket embroidered in the Dene Nation of Northwest Territories, Canada

Reconnecting to Expression

The practice of stitching meaning into textiles has continued for millennia, and while many Indigenous communities hold tightly to their traditions, much of the history of embroidered symbolism is lost—along with the embroideries themselves. Fabric has a way of turning into dust over just a few centuries.

> When we choose to stitch onto our textiles, we're creating an opportunity to develop a more intimate relationship with the objects that surround us, while preserving an ancient tradition.

Though most textiles are lost to time, symbolism in design exists everywhere. Gargoyle statues on the tops of buildings represent protection. They may not literally guard the building, but sculptors have captured that essence and desire. Painted flames on the side of a car are not actually making that car go any faster, but they represent what the driver wishes to embody—a ride so fast the tires leave you in the smoke! Design uncovers what is important to us and brings clarity to what we want.

Connecting to Ancestry

Research the stitches of your own family lineage. If you don't connect with or know your blood ancestry, then look at a chosen lineage you're drawn to. You might ask family elders, grandparents or parents, aunts and uncles, about their own memories of any embroidery within the family. Have any embroidered heirlooms been passed down? You might dive into the textile history of your ancestral or chosen lineage at a local library, or ask around at local antique shops, or even scour the internet for vintage dealers, museum archives, and other collections. Take care to be respectful of minority cultures that you do not belong to, and avoid directly copying symbols and imagery.

* What imagery stands out to you?

* If the object is wearable, what areas of the cloth were embellished?

* Record each example in your sketchbook, drawing out the overall effect of the embroidery.

* Observe the stitches closely and draw the texture of each.

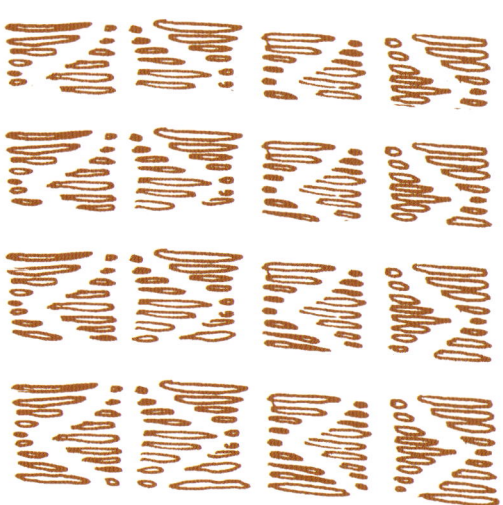

If you aren't familiar with the stitches you see, refer to Stitch Methods (starting on page 159) for identification.

Stitching from Tradition

Using the stitches you identified in your sketchbook or choosing ones highlighted in the inspiring examples on pages 22–51, select two to practice in the first and second positions of your sampler. Keep it simple if it's your first time trying these stitches. Test making a series of horizontal lines or filling in a small basic shape like a square or triangle.

Clockwise from top left, these practice samples show herringbone stitch, running stitch, straight stitches alongside a blanket stitch wheel, and open chain stitch.

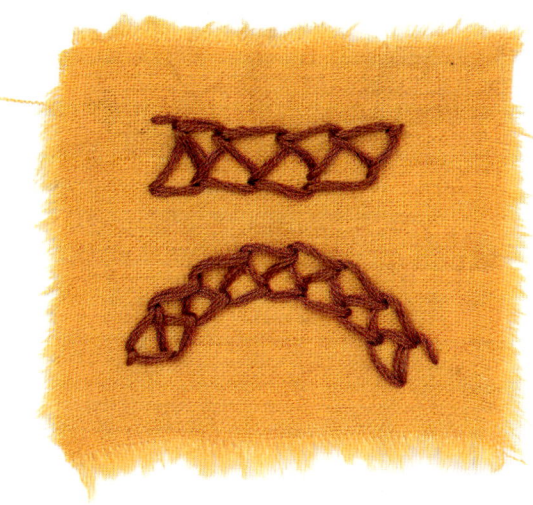

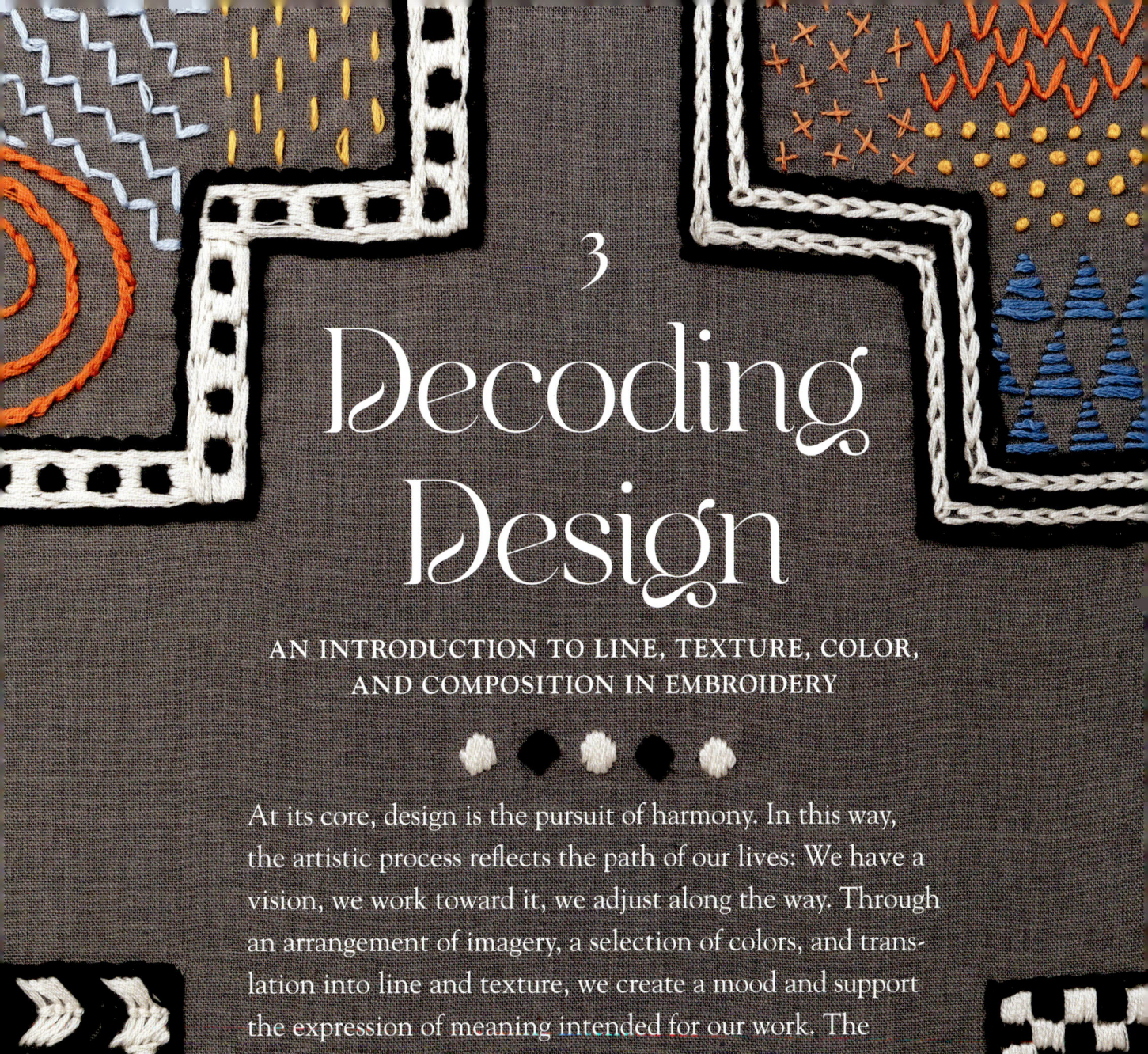

3
Decoding Design

AN INTRODUCTION TO LINE, TEXTURE, COLOR, AND COMPOSITION IN EMBROIDERY

At its core, design is the pursuit of harmony. In this way, the artistic process reflects the path of our lives: We have a vision, we work toward it, we adjust along the way. Through an arrangement of imagery, a selection of colors, and translation into line and texture, we create a mood and support the expression of meaning intended for our work. The results are not always as we imagined, but the act of continually envisioning, creating, and adjusting brings us closer to our desired outcome each time.

Principles of Design

The study of design often uncovers principles or elements that are based on observing the natural world—the ultimate creation. For the sake of simplicity, we'll focus on the elements of design most obvious in embroidery:

* Line
* Texture
* Color
* Composition

Concepts such as contrast, movement, pattern, symmetry, and proportion are interwoven with these elements, which we'll experience through projects that encourage the exploration of materials and concepts.

Theories of design do not necessarily come naturally to everyone, but style does. As we explore our own style through our sketchbook—looking at what we choose to surround ourselves with in our homes, and where we find our eyes lingering out in the world—we develop our own language with the alphabet of design.

> In studying elements of design, you'll eventually find yourself in opposition to a theory. Don't subscribe to design rules and absolutes that don't work for you.

To Plan or Not to Plan

The choice to plan a design or go freestyle depends on the project at hand, your own personality, and the desired final product. If you just want to explore and can handle a bit of contained chaos, freestyling might be just what you need to expand your creative horizons. That choice should affect your expectations, though. High expectations with no advance plan are a recipe for disappointment. Not to plan is to approach the work with a deep curiosity, like a scientist who knows there's a good chance their experiment might fail but chooses the risk of failure over predictability.

So, what if we do want to plan? How do we go about doing this? Using colored pencils or markers is helpful, or even cutting little pieces of your chosen colors (for more on this, see page 104). Alternatively—and one of my favorite methods—use the "markup" tool on your cell phone, or any app that lets you draw on photos. Being able to take a photo of the fabric, sketch, or final garment I'm working with and use my finger to quickly scribble in general composition and color notes (and erase just as quickly) has become my go-to mode of planning. Just try your best not to get side-tracked by the dozens of distractions now at your fingertips!

After drawing the basic outline on the fabric, I sketched three versions of this quilt-inspired star to play with line weight and emphasis, landing on the final version to stitch, keeping the focus at the center of the image.

Reading the Materials

No matter how highly developed our designs are and how much detail we've developed, the materials will often dictate how the work will go. Testing new fabrics, threads, or stitch methods before investing a significant amount of energy deciding what you want them to do will often save you loads of time!

Experimenting in advance introduces ease and flow into the work. A thick metallic thread will not succumb easily to small stitches and sharp turns. A thin, flowing silk fabric will not support the thickness of a thousand bulky threads. Test needle and thread on either a scrap of fabric or an unseen corner of the final fabric or garment. Work with their tendencies and adjust your designs accordingly.

Velvets, satins, and dense, lightweight, or sheer fabrics can be challenging to embroider.

"But I Don't Know How to Draw!"

There might be a feeling of extreme distance between our capabilities and our desire to create. If you have little to no experience drawing, I recommend starting with basic shapes, such as squares, circles, and triangles. Most of what we develop when creating imagery is composed of the same elements that make up the basic shapes. Even an amorphous squiggly blob is essentially the curves of a circle folding in and out.

Drawing is not all about imitating lifelike forms. Many artists work exclusively with forms that fall outside the realm of reality—like the imagined shapes of Henri Matisse, the playfully imperfect figures and perspective of Faith Ringgold, and the geometric arrangements of much of the embroidered art shared in the previous chapter.

These snakes are simply lines of alternating color with heads.

Trusting Intuition
with Elizabeth Pawle

I'm often asked how I plan my pieces and I always give the same answer: I don't! For me, drawing or planning a piece takes away the intuition I pull from when I stitch and spoils the enjoyment I take from watching a design appear in front of me.

I start by cutting a piece of burlap and pulling together a bundle of yarns from the huge stash I keep. I tend to stick to rainbow colors with lots of bright shades and neons, and I also include a number of yarns I've dyed myself, in a variety of weights from fine mohair threads to squishy super-chunky wools.

Toward the beginning of each piece I tend to grab my colors and weight of yarn at random, only starting to pay closer attention to what yarn I'm using and where I'm adding it as the tapestry becomes more densely packed.

I tend to work very quickly and I listen to music while I stitch, which helps to keep my mind from overthinking the project in front of me. I've become good at knowing when my piece is finished—something that only comes from practice, I think—and I rarely go back to add extra details."

Elizabeth Pawle's
PRO TIP
If you feel you can't draw, I highly recommend skipping that part and jumping straight in with needle and thread. Make some marks and see what appears! It really is that simple.

Using Geometry as Your Scaffolding

This technique is for those of us who swear we cannot draw! Getting out of your head and turning your focus onto the paper, trace circles from small bottles, jar lids, rolls of tape, spools of thread, buttons, coins, or anything else cylindrical that can become a stencil. Likewise, anything with corners can be the beginning of repetitive sharp angles. No two collections of objects will be the same. The way you put the shapes together will be unique to you.

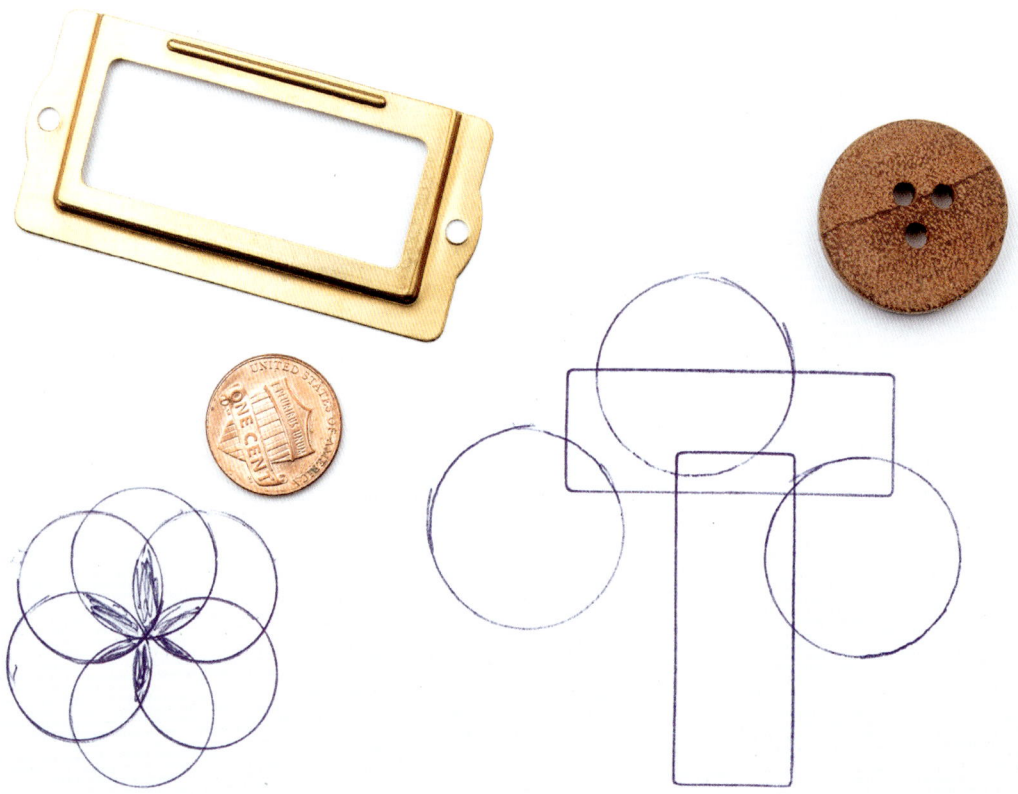

The magic of embroidery is that once these lines are translated into stitches, they come to life, both for yourself and for all who will see the piece.

Step into more intricate shapes like clothespins and scissors. Take a trip through the junk drawer and just grab a pile of different objects. Begin to trace their outlines onto scrap paper. Draw in pen or marker, unerasable, and experience a special sort of freedom from perfection.

Working with thin, cheap copy paper allows you to easily trace what you've already drawn to create repetitive patterns. Connect shapes, intersect them, fill them with textures.

Line

So inherent in design that we nearly overlook it, line is the beginning of shape and form. Every embroidered work combines short lines to create larger motifs. Even the uniform, smooth texture of an area covered in satin stitch is composed of parallel lines. Choices around materials and stitch methods create a variety of effects and open the opportunity for more dimensional works of art.

Exploring Line Character

Starting from a single point and moving in any direction, line is the beginning of shape and form. When we look at the waves of color stitched on this pages, we begin to see how a line isn't always simply a line. Depending on the stitch chosen, the line is a delicate undulation, a bold presence, or a smooth, silky flow. My choice of backstitch, chain stitch, or stem stitch contributes greatly to the overall impact of the composition.

Exploring Line Weight

Since the stitches in the previous example differ in both texture and line weight, let's reduce the variables. By nature, the backstitch is only a simple line, but changing the weight of the thread allows you to create different intensities. The elements of your design begin to step off the fabric, taking on more depth than if all the lines were the same weight.

Take for example this flowing water. The difference in line weight is very subtle, but we see the thicker lines on the border as a definite edge, while the thinner lines, created with fewer and fewer strands of the six-strand embroidery floss, serve to describe the movement of the water and not an edge.

As you explore how to incorporate line into your own design, study how each option affects the energy of its space. Consider concepts of movement or stillness, boldness or subtlety, flatness or depth, chaos or order. How can line character and weight, outside of representing an object or a space, contribute to the overall impact of a design?

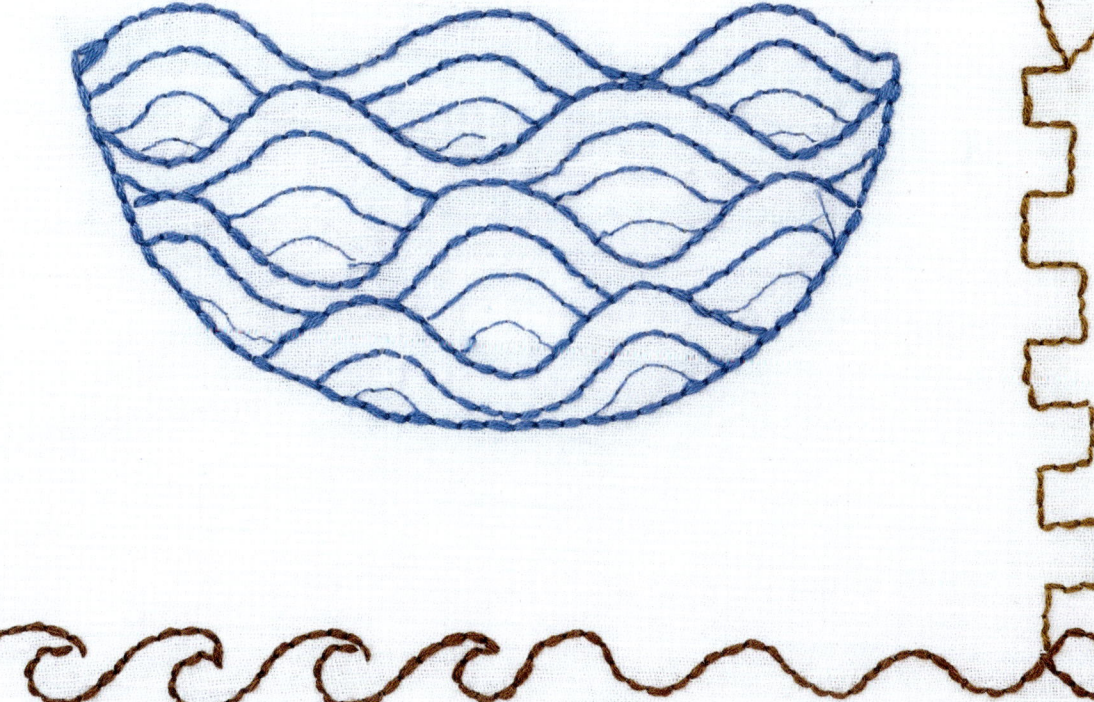

Celebrating Doodles
with Rebecca Ringquist

For my business, Dropcloth Samplers, I design and sell sampler patterns and other embroidery projects. Each design is more open-ended than a traditional pattern, leaving room for stitchers to customize as they go and make the finished piece their own.

Almost always, my inspiration for new designs comes from sketchbook doodles. I usually have four or five books going at once, and if I find myself without one in the wild, I'll glue drawings in later. Usually an idea goes from a little doodle to a slightly better drawing to a finished drawing on bristol paper that will eventually become a printed design for embroidery.

I am a very intuitive embroiderer. I love to make up the color palette as I go, pulling from my stash to balance out colors as needed. Being open to experimentation is crucial to my practice in other ways, too. Just like you can draw with a mechanical pencil or a thick, juicy marker, you can embroider with all different weights of thread. Sometimes a thin embroidered line made of sewing thread is just perfect. Other times a fluffy knitting yarn will work better for the mood I'm trying to create."

Rebecca Ringquist's
PRO TIP
Backstitch, chain stitch, French knots, and couching make up 80 percent of my work, but I like backstitch the most because it's so versatile. This plain old line can be text, drawings, outlines…GEEZ it even looks good outlining itself in another color!

Designing with Straight Lines

Embroidery is made up of single straight lines. You cannot stitch a curved shape without using a series of straight lines. Play with compositional arrangements made entirely of straight lines in your sketchbook. Not sure how to do this?

* Play with varying line lengths, working the lines in patterns like rows and columns.
* Crisscross them over one another.

* Allow them to radiate out from a center.
* Create a flowing movement.
* Scatter them randomly.

Look back at some of your drawings in previous pages of your sketchbook for a boost of inspiration.

Try to keep these arrangements small, a few inches or so in size. The goal is to practice multiple arrangements and discover what you like and don't like, not to perfect one. Do not erase the ones you don't like—these may come in handy later, if only as an example of what not to do.

SPLITTING YOUR THREAD

Embroidery floss is made up of six strands that you can split into two, three, four, or even single strands. To split your thread, cut a length of floss to about an arm's length, or up to 1 yard (36 inches). At one end, separate the amount you want. Slowly and gently—to avoid tangles—tease the two sections apart down the length of the strands.

Stitching with Straight Lines

Stitch your favorite compositions from the two experiments Using Geometry as Your Scaffolding (page 64) and Designing with Straight Lines (opposite) in the third and fourth positions of your sampler using simple straight stitches.

These are some favorites from what I sketched. What will your designs look like?

Texture

With the element of texture, we move from
creating an outline or edge to detailing a surface
area. Even using only the most basic stitches, we
can find excitingly chaotic textures, soothingly
gentle textures, and everything in between.

There's an inherent relationship between the
sense of touch and texture. Though we can see
texture, it is often associated with physically
handling an object—something to keep in mind
when working with a tactile art like embroidery.

Exploring Spacing

As a series of separate lines that allow for infinite expression, the running stitch becomes an ideal exploration of textural options. Note how the spacing of not only the rows of stitching but also the stitches themselves influences the overall effect. By going back in with stitches in the other direction and connecting rows of running stitch, we've got a whole new selection of geometric arrangements to explore as well.

As a way of implying form through a collection of lines, texture in embroidery can fill an area without requiring dense stitches. Take for example the rays emanating from the top of this eye. Though they cover very little surface area, in our minds their texture and rhythm read as a filled area. Close rows of running stitch in the rays below the eye create a dense yet still textured fill for a very different effect.

With a line of running stitch, you can space the stitches closer or farther apart for different effects. You can also space the lines densely or loosely.

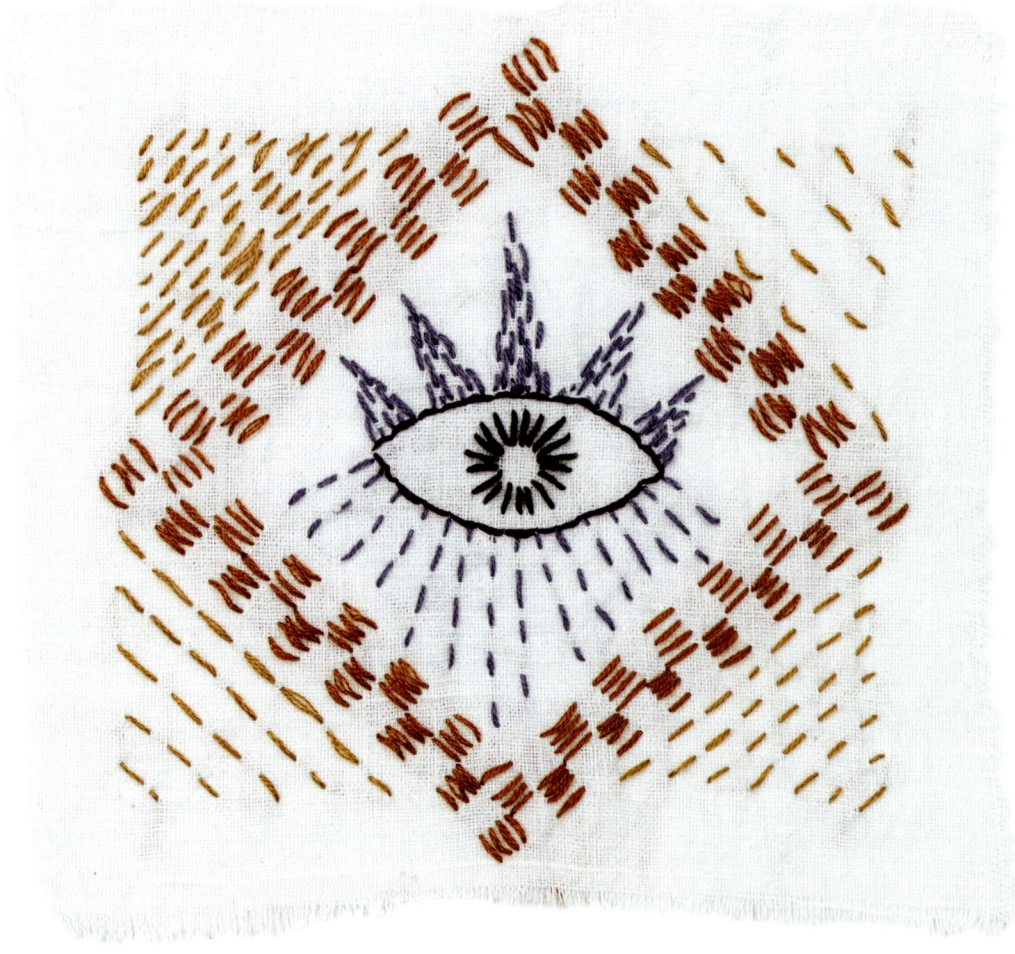

TEXTURE LIBRARY

From smooth and solid to stripes and dashes, the way you choose to fill a shape should either reflect the texture of the form you're representing or allow it to stand out from the other shapes within your design.

Nearly all stitches can be isolated in some way and used to create texture, but these are some of my favorite options. Check out one or many; mix and match for textural delight!

Stitch Key

- **A** running stitch
- **B** star stitch
- **C** grid stitch
- **D** French knots
- **E** detached chain stitch
- **F** seed stitch (overlapping)
- **G** herringbone stitch
- **H** fly stitch
- **I** blanket stitch
- **J** straight stitch (overlapping)
- **K** seed stitch
- **L** blanket stitch (overlapping)

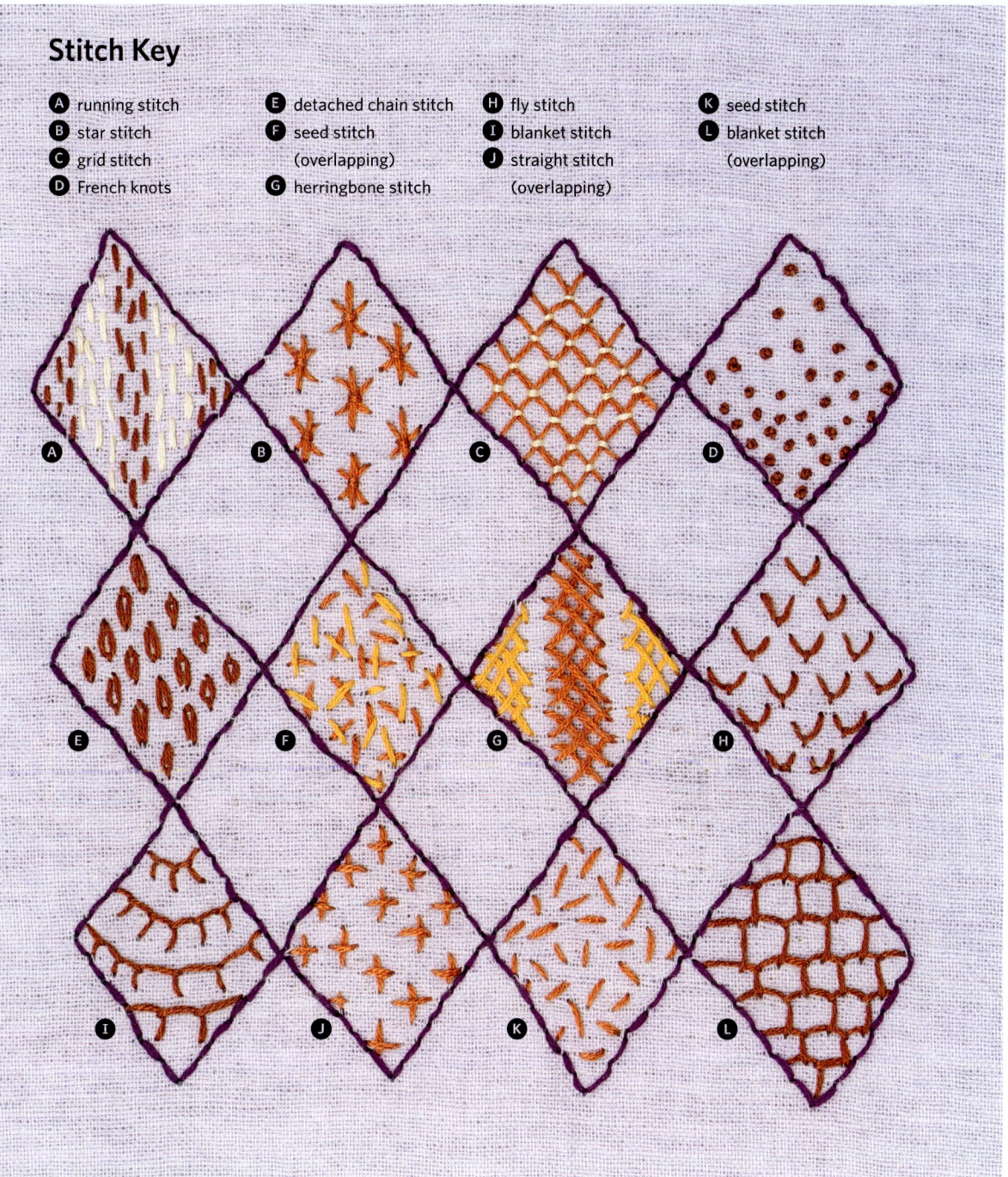

Infinite Stitching
with Gabriela Martínez Ortiz

We are surrounded, wherever we live, by an endless number of patterns with rhythms of repetition. We see them in the printed pages of a book, on the streets, in a building, on our clothes, or in the sky. I consider myself a pattern-finder, especially in nature. Whenever I feel stuck, I try to go there, admiring a tree, the water, a leaf, or a landscape.

In my work, I explore the concept of infinity. Applying organic dots and lines in numerous quantities achieves visual movement that invites contemplation. Embroidering in this way is also a meditative tool for me. I can access a trance by doing the same movements over and over again.

I sketch on paper what I want to highlight in a pattern to understand the strength of the texture that I imagine applying repeatedly—always looking to take that pattern to the extreme. From there, I see what happens when the hand is allowed to be free and textures appear from the repetition of organic forms, without a rigid plan or rules. Letting intuition be the guide as I stitch allows me to create the unimaginable."

Gabriela Martínez Ortiz's
PRO TIP
Questioning why I like what I like has been key in developing my creative language. By collecting images that attract me and studying the relationships between them, I realize if I like orderly or disorderly, colorful or neutral, geometric or organic, etc.

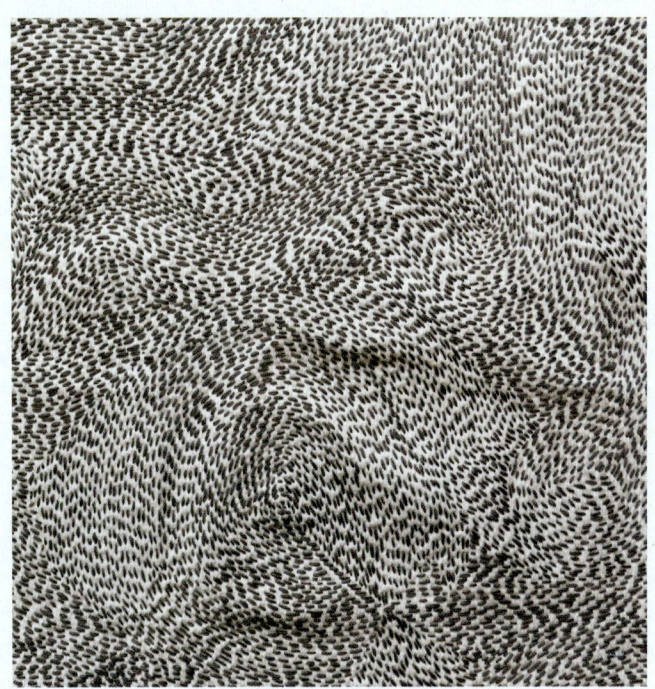

Exploring Density and Direction

As a variation of spacing, you can express the darkness and lightness of a form through the density or the direction of stitches. Vary the distance between stitches in order to create darker and lighter forms—like the airy feel of the top green leaf, or the thick, solid presence of the bottom purple leaf (both created using rows of running stitch). You can mix these airy stitches with denser stitches to create the feeling of shading.

Beyond the running stitch, notice the satin stitch leaves on the right stem. Consider how a series of diagonal lines might give a different effect than a series of horizontal lines. Take the time to visualize, and even sketch out, the finished effect before stitching.

The flowers on the top of the design show just a few options for filling an area with texture in varying levels of density—from left to right, satin stitch, chain stitch, running stitch, and seed stitch.

Stitching on top of stitches adds an unexpected density to the texture, making the stitches even more three-dimensional. For example, layer a running stitch or detached chain stitch over an area of satin stitches, as in the leaf on the bottom left. You might also choose to stitch small motifs first, then fill the surrounding area with satin stitch, creating a dense textural impact with a little less thickness, as in the leaf on the bottom right.

Achieving Flow
with Lindzeanne

I really like outer space and cosmic imagery in general. I love to look at NASA Hubble telescope images. It's interesting how we can see the literal flow of energy of those faraway places, and we see that same flow here on Earth—in aerial views of rivers, for example. Like celestial bodies, there is a push and pull between shapes in my work. I like to think about balance and weight.

I don't typically plan a design. I'm an impatient person with a busy mind. I choose a certain point in a piece to be the center of gravity, like a starting point. And then, as if you were moving your hand through water or drawing a pattern in the sand, that is the general movement of the thread, moving out and away from that center of gravity. It's imprecise.

I don't unpick stitches. If I feel like I have made a mistake, I just keep going with the flow. I'm too impatient to make edits, and often if I fuss with a piece, I lose the initial feeling or image I was trying capture in the first place."

Lindzeanne's
PRO TIP
When in doubt, keep adding more. A piece feels finished when the weight of it is satisfying to me and makes me want to run my hand over it. I am a very tactile person.

Designing Texture

Study the anatomy of your favorite flower. How do you describe its curves and undulations in your stitches? Do the edges feel dimensional and textured or smooth? How might you illustrate the color variations using line and texture? Don't limit yourself to the outline; consider how long parallel lines, overlapping short lines, or tiny dot stitches within the shape might give your petals more dimension.

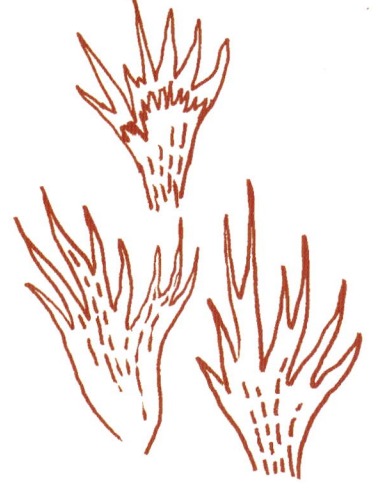

I've sketched the petals of some of my favorite flowers. What flowers speak to you?

Stitching Texture

In the fifth position of your sampler, use the backstitch to embroider some flower petals. Go beyond outlining the edges. If we look closely at a sunflower petal, for example, we'll see that it is deeply ridged with vertical lines. A peony petal has a highly ruffled outer edge. Explore the texture closely and stitch the minute details. Consider this a detailed study of the petal's surface as described through line. You don't need to fit the whole flower into the space. You may want to split your thread so you're only using two or three strands of a six-ply embroidery floss.

In the sixth position of your sampler, create a texture using running stitch that implies shading. Play with the length of the stitch, how close or far away the stitches are from one another, and which direction the stitches are heading. Are the stitches parallel to one another? Do they overlap? Do the stitches radiate from a single point?

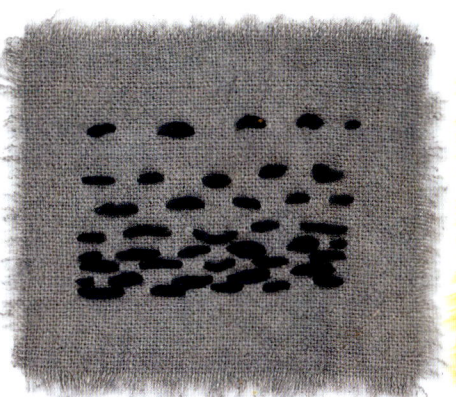

Color

The way the eye receives color is deeply connected to feelings and emotions. We are naturally drawn to or repelled by certain colors based on how they make us feel. Let's explore what color is made of and methods of choosing color palettes for your piece that reflect its deeper meaning while also delighting the eye.

Exploring Color Perception

Our choice of color brings an added dimension to the meaning we weave with threads. Consider the use of the word in the common phrase "to *color* someone's experience," meaning to *influence* someone's perception. Our emotional interpretation of an image is heavily influenced by the colors chosen. For instance, we might choose a monochromatic palette for subtle shifts, or high-contrast vibrancy to sing our objectives loudly.

> Color does not live in isolation; it exists in relationship to its surroundings.

When we see color, our eyes receive wavelengths of light reflecting off an object. Our brains then interpret these wavelengths, often shifting the translation slightly to read color more clearly against other colors. A golden yellow on a dark brown background will read to our minds differently from the same golden yellow on a pale lavender background.

Our life experiences also influence our perception of color. How many times have you seen a color combination that seemed nearly offensive to you, yet someone you know and love placed those colors together because it was pleasing to them?

The small red squares within the navy and yellow backgrounds appear to be different shades of red, but they are exactly the same color. Our eye works to better differentiate the yellow background from the red square by making it appear darker.

We see the same happening with the green squares. Our eyes perceive a darker green on the lighter background, and a lighter green on the darker background, even though the greens are in fact the same.

Hue is the spectrum of basic colors that you see in a rainbow.

Exploring Color Components

While a deep study of color is not necessary to begin creating your own color palettes, understanding the elements of color allows you to choose a palette much more confidently. The following section—as always in this book—offers avenues of exploration, not rules and requirements. With that in mind, let's explore each component of what a color is made of: hue, value, and saturation.

Hue is how we describe pure color without any white, gray, or black added. Primary red, yellow, and blue are hues, as well as every mixture of them in between: a bright red with a touch of yellow like the petals of a poppy flower, or a blue with a touch of red, dancing the line between royal and ultraviolet.

When describing the hue of a given color, we are attempting to see beyond how light or dark or bright or dull the color is and describe only the amounts of red, yellow, and blue (in whatever combination) that exist in the color.

Value describes the highs and lows of a hue, or changes in lightness and darkness. As yellow gets darker and darker, it moves through ocher and then into shades of umber brown. As red lightens up, it turns into a shade better known as pink. When we are embroidering areas of shading from light to dark, we usually want to find colors of different value. I often take this opportunity to find colors that shift in hue as well.

Monotone colors are darker and lighter values of the same hue.

Changing both value and hue tends to add vibrancy, highlighting that area of the design.

Saturation expresses the intensity of a hue. The higher the saturation, the more intense a color is. The lower the saturation, the closer it is to gray. Through desaturating a color, green turns to olive, purple transforms into mauve, and blue becomes slate.

These dusty colors often help to visually push colors back in a composition. Painters use saturation in a technique called "atmospheric perspective," where the background of a landscape will be grayer (and often bluer in hue) in an attempt to add dimension to a flat plane. Shades of color that are less saturated allow brighter colors to pop off the page, while also toning down the overall palette of the piece.

A wide range of colors is available before a hue is fully desaturated to gray.

Improvising Color
with Sarah K. Benning

There are color combinations that I gravitate toward, like working with complementary colors, but I don't plan out a full palette for my pieces. I usually just choose a color to get started and make each additional color choice based off of the previous selection. The great thing about embroidery is that it is quite flexible. If I ever make a color choice I don't like, I can simply cut it out and try again.

This year, I have started recording particular color combinations that I like so I can come back to them for future projects. Usually this happens pretty spontaneously when I notice random combinations within piles of thread in the studio. I cut samples from the group and tape and label them in a notebook.

I believe it is possible to create really compelling work using just a few techniques. I use long satin stitches to create fields of color and rely on drawing and the careful composition of my pieces to bring in complexity. I am not personally interested in pushing the thread to behave like a different medium such as paint. I'm working with it because it is thread and I like the textures and surfaces it creates on its own."

Sarah Benning's
PRO TIP
I find that black outlines make my pieces feel more finished and decisive. On a practical level, the black line cleans up the imperfect edges of my satin stitch and clarifies shapes and detail.

Moving Across the Color Globe

The relationship between colors is often studied in a two-dimensional illustration called a color wheel, but I prefer to use a color globe, which models hue, value, and saturation simultaneously.

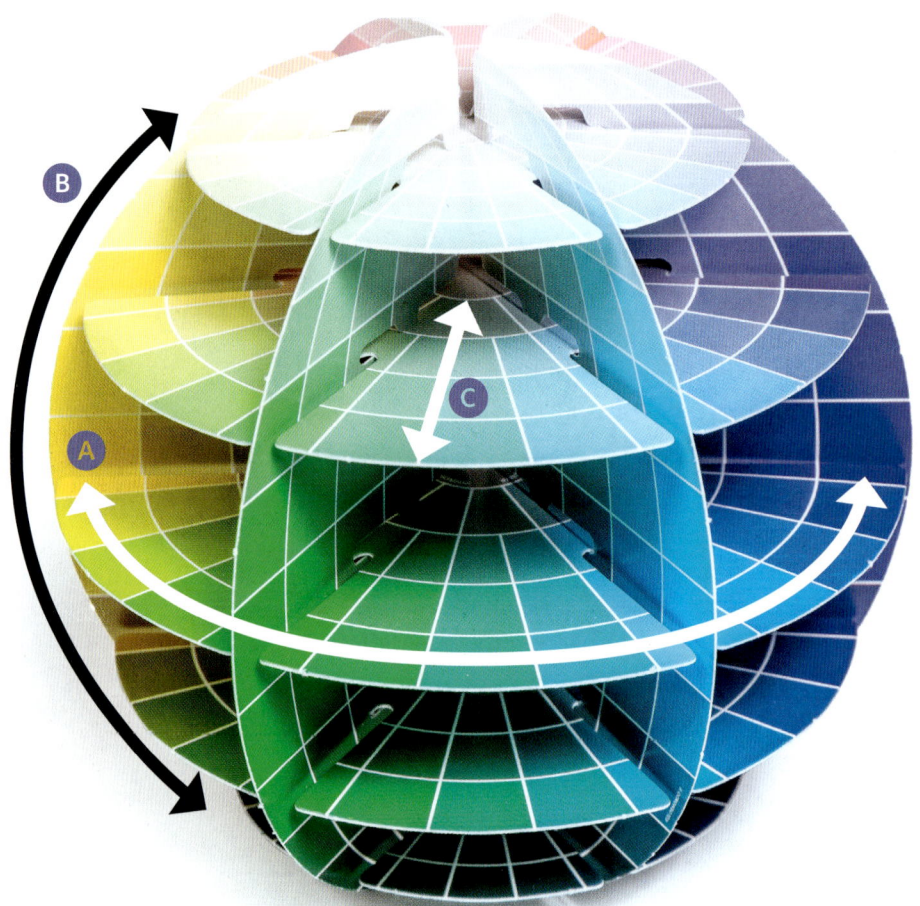

A Hue changes as you travel around the globe.

B Value changes as you travel up and down the globe.

C Saturation changes as you move into the globe.

Why does this matter? Understanding what makes up a color allows us to play with combinations in more exciting ways that seem to visually pop the stitches off the fabric. Use these subtle nuances and variances in unexpected combinations to draw the eye in and around your work of art.

Monotone colors are the same hue, in darker and lighter shades, or values. The flower petal shown is simply light pink, medium pink, and dark pink. Colors have been selected from the color globe within a single longitudinal line for a monotone effect. While a beautiful way of filling in this petal, what if we took a more dynamic approach to choosing these colors? What if we not only moved up and down the color globe, but also left and right?

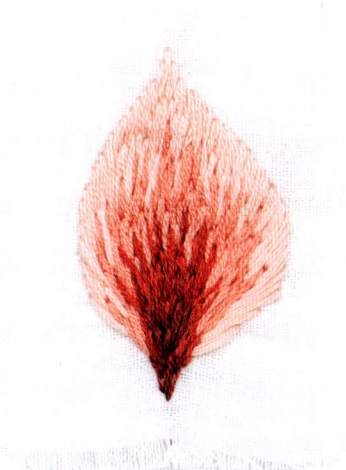

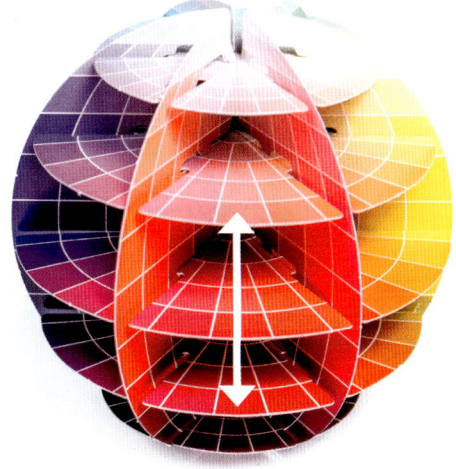

The thread selections for this flower petal follow a single longitudinal line on the color globe.

Analogous colors are hues that lie next to one another on the color globe. These are usually a safe bet when creating harmony within a palette. Our next flower petal starts from a pale pink that is a little more orange in hue, moves to a pure bright pink, and finishes with a dark pink that is a little more purple. These colors still sit next to one another on the globe, and they give the petal an almost electric quality.

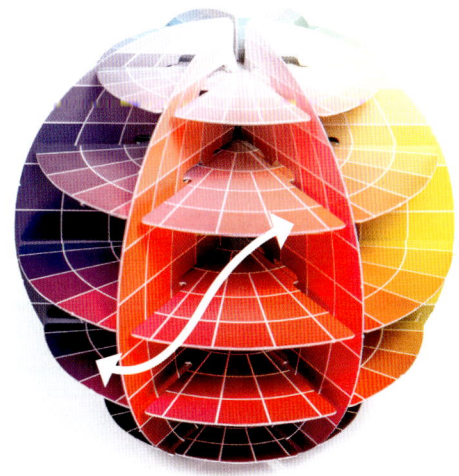

These thread selections move down the color globe but also across it to adjacent hues.

Complementary colors lie opposite one another on the globe and are so often misunderstood! Just because bright yellow is opposite bright purple doesn't necessarily mean they will *complement*, or enhance, each other. What I do is look at the desaturated, or grayer, shade of the opposite color.

If I'm starting with a bright purple, I might pair it with a desaturated yellow, a sort of bronze-gray, as a contrast. To the same degree, if I have a bright yellow, a dusty lavender is going to be my first choice. Purple and yellow are one of my favorite combos, though I very rarely use them together in full saturation as pure hues. Dusty dark indigo with red or orange stitching is an example of complementary colors that we see regularly in denim. We also see the opposite—bright blue enhances a rusty orange.

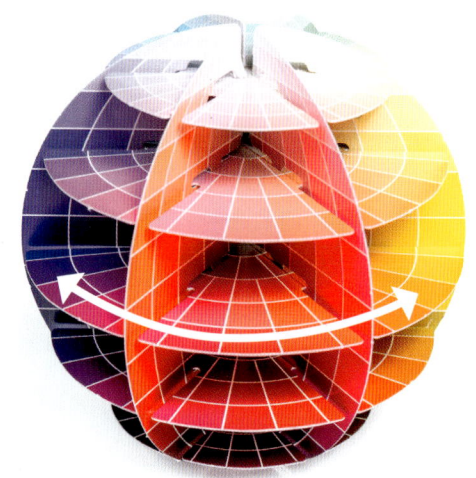

I selected these thread colors from opposite sides of the color globe.

TRUST YOURSELF

Don't feel the need to depend on the color globe. Using color systems to choose every color in a palette is a bit like using a thesaurus to find every word for an entire sentence.

Instead, use these systems like you would a thesaurus; write your poetry, then consult the color systems to find more poetic hues after intuition has led the selection.

Planning Your Own Palette

As you work with color more intimately, you start to develop a natural feeling for the color combinations that work well in your eye, versus those that might be a little less agreeable to you. Noticing the colors that you already chose for your wardrobe and home is a great way to identify favorite themes as a starting point.

If planning the palette for a project isn't feeling intuitive, I find the following formula to be helpful: I make sure I have one light, one dark, one bright, and a range of three colors that form shading—whether those are monotone colors, analogous colors, or complementary colors. The previous three requirements of light, dark, and bright might exist within these shades.

I don't always stick to this formula. Sometimes all you need is one or two colors to make an embroidery impactful. Sometimes you need a dozen. I do, however, keep track of the colors I am drawn to. I record them in a notebook, taping a few inches of thread to the page with an annotation of the color number. Once you've identified the colors you love, then start purchasing more colors in that range so you'll have shading options. Over time, you'll develop a library of colors that work well with your style and have your own personal palette!

One light, one dark, and a range of three colors that form shading is usually a winning formula.

BEWARE OF DIGITAL COLOR

If you plan to buy threads online, be aware that photos of embroidery floss on a backlit screen don't accurately represent the true color of the physical thread. Just because you pick a light blue, a medium blue, and a dark blue, it doesn't mean they will work well together. Every hue has a wide range, and a greenish blue might clash against a purplish blue. If I don't already have what I need, I often go to a brick-and-mortar store so I can see how colors look together. That way I know what I love in real life. Then if I want to purchase online, I can easily do that using the number on the skein.

Testing Color Choices

Since the way your eye reads a color depends on the colors around it, seeing the threads you choose on the fabric you'll be embroidering is important. Unwind a few rounds of the embroidery floss to see how a small strip of the color will appear. Seeing the entire skein of thread against the fabric may look different from seeing a single thread, which is closer to the actual effect when you stitch. Laying your options out in good lighting is also important. Daylight is always best.

Artist Pacita Abad's trapunto paintings illustrate how color choices strongly impact even similar compositions.

On the facing page we see the same palette on three different colors of fabric. Notice how the impact of the colors changes drastically depending on the background.

Unexpected Color Crescendo

While blending colors that sit close together on the color globe allows for a delicate cascade of colors, blending colors that contrast with one another helps achieve surprisingly delightful results. If a shading of colors is feeling a little bland, sometimes the best thing to liven up the stitches is to go in with a contrasting color. Play around with different saturations and add some excitement!

Try mixing opposing colors using satin stitch. You may find that separating the threads down to two or three strands allows for a more delicate blending within the stark contrast.

Above are three examples of the same petal, stitched with six strands of thread on the left, four strands of thread in the center, and two strands on the right.

The longer petals below all have contrasting colors stitched through to give a more luminous effect.

MIXING COLORS

We can't mix colors with thread in the same way we do with paint, but we can play with how they sit next to each other. Subtle variances in hue, value, and saturation make certain parts of our embroideries feel as though they were mixed paints. The long and short satin stitch has the most painterly effect, allowing us to blend two colors so it almost appears as though an entirely new color has been created. By splitting our thread to three, two, or even one strand, even more delicate blends are possible.

Variegated thread, in which the color of the thread transitions along the length of the floss, is another way of mixing colors as we stitch, adding an exciting element of chance.

See page 102 to learn about the art of Beth Hoyes.

Studying Nature
with Beth Hoyes

I love the incredible range of color in nature and how a creature or plant may only seem to be a couple of colors from a distance but is a whole host of hues, tones, and textures when you look closely.

The process of stitching color with thread reminds me of pointillism in painting. The colors blend together through proximity and relate to each other for an overall effect. On a practical level, I blend either by layering different colors or by stitching gradients in which colors go from lighter to darker or warmer to colder, for example. In my experience, layers of straight stitch are best for following the natural flow of colors and add much to the texture of the embroidery as well.

Unless I'm making patterns for others to follow, I'm not a planner when it comes to color. I print or sketch the outlines of a design onto fabric, then spontaneously add stitches of different colors in various areas of the design, using a photo or a specimen such as a feather for reference. Often the piece looks like a hot mess for a long time while I work with little riots of scattered color. There is something so sweet about when it all comes together in the end."

Beth Hoyes's
PRO TIP
Thinner thread is always helpful for details and subtle changes. I often find the thinner the thread, the more subtle color detail and complex blends I can create.

Designing with Color

Take all the thread options you have and snip a few 2" pieces off each. Create three to five color stories on background swatches of fabric or paper in different shades, using the following color palette formula:

* ✳ one light
* ✳ one dark
* ✳ one bright
* ✳ a range of three colors that form shading

Haven't got much in thread color options? Cut out 10 to 20 different color squares from a magazine, and slice a few ¼" strips of each. Now create different combinations of shades with these. Glue or tape these palettes down in pleasing arrangements in your sketchbook.

Stitching with Color

Color Blocking. In the seventh position of your sampler, fill in a shape with three adjacent strips of color. I used herringbone and Bokhara couching stitches for these examples, as I thought they'd provide a nice bit of texture while also creating a solid block of color, but you could also try chain stitch or even split stitch to do this experiment.

Color Mixing. Choose three colors at random, maybe even with your eyes closed. In the eighth position of your sampler, use the long and short stitch to blend them into a flower petal. Which combinations offend you? Which combinations are you surprisingly drawn to? If you find the colors aren't blending to your liking, it may help to split the threads down to two or three strands.

Here are some examples of color blocking (at left) and color mixing (above).

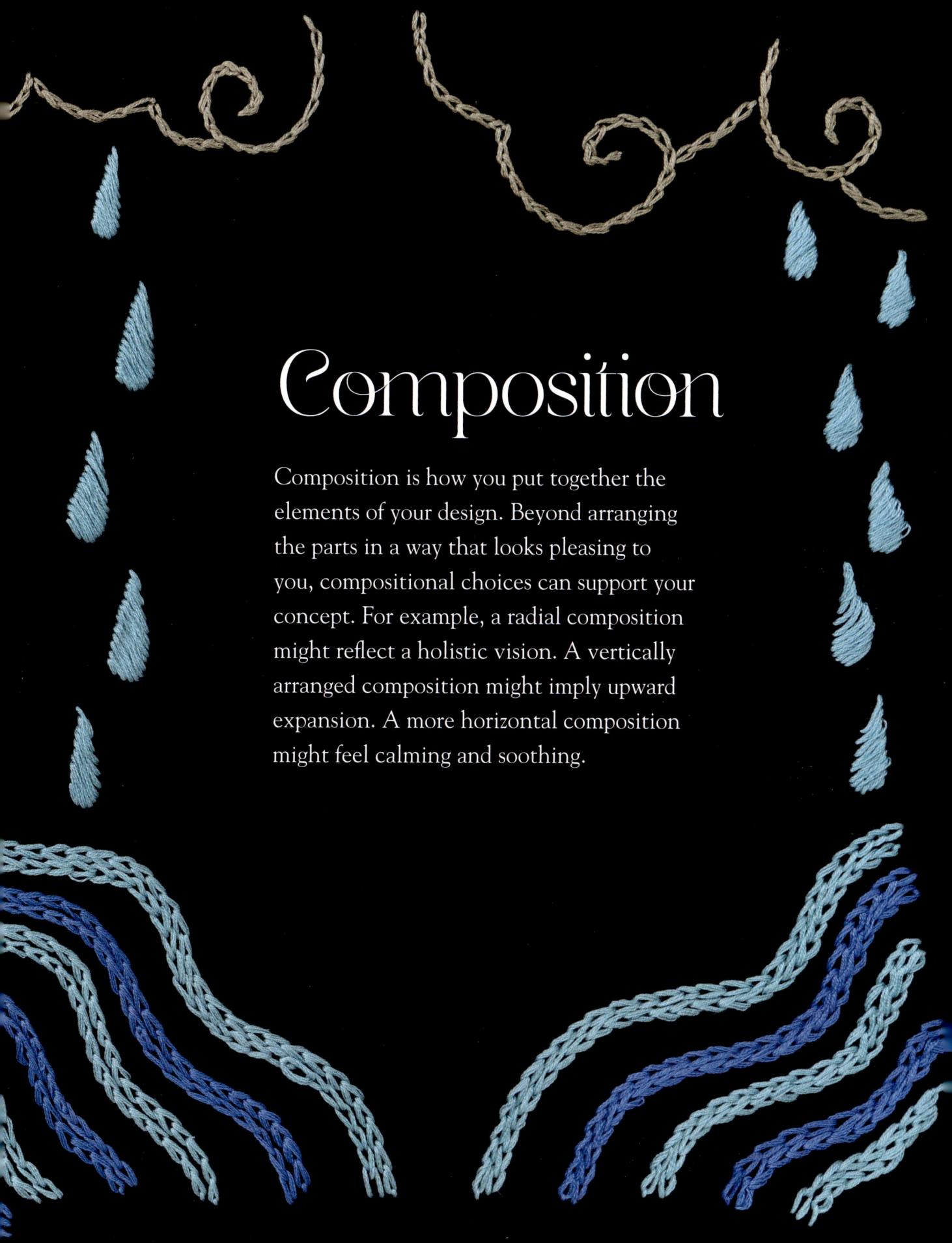

Composition

Composition is how you put together the elements of your design. Beyond arranging the parts in a way that looks pleasing to you, compositional choices can support your concept. For example, a radial composition might reflect a holistic vision. A vertically arranged composition might imply upward expansion. A more horizontal composition might feel calming and soothing.

Planning a Composition

When you have some sketches that you're excited to embroider, you are ready to translate them into a full-scale composition. Exploring concepts of space, balance, movement, pattern, symmetry, emphasis, and proportion, you can refine sketches and combine design elements by photocopying, tracing, or sketching onto scrap paper with bold markers. (I keep a pile of junk mail that has been printed only on one side just for this kind of work!)

Place your design on the garment or fabric or whatever you're developing this artwork for. Move it around to find the ideal position. If there are multiple motifs, try placing the elements in different arrangements and snap photos for comparison. If you intend to embroider something that you'll wear—whatever you do—*put the garment on* with these sketches pinned in place before you do any stitching! Consider the curves of the body and how you'll move in this garment. Are you doing your best to give this design a great location? Does the scale complement your form?

Space

To let lines, forms, and textures stand out from one another, negative space is required. Negative space is the part of the design where seemingly nothing happens, yet it has such a strong influence on the overall effect. One of my main rules when designing an embroidery is to allow space to be an integral part of the composition. Not only do I avoid spending 10,000 hours finishing a piece, I also find the design becomes more dynamic.

Instead of large areas of solid forms, might you create an open texture using rows of running stitch, for example, saving many hours of work? Or do you in fact love stitching with dense detail?

The fish and cloud on the left are stitched with dense, solid areas, while the same forms on the right allow the background fabric to become part of the design. When working with colored fabrics, I find that including negative space becomes even more effective at creating harmony within a composition.

Balance

Balance is a method of arranging design elements harmoniously by distributing the "weight" of the image equally. Symmetry is not required, though symmetrical designs are a form of balance. In the example shown here, I've balanced the twirling vine on the right with shapes that take up a similar amount of space, and imply a similar undulation of curves, on the opposite side of the image. If your intention is to create a feeling of unity or harmony, having a balanced design might support this goal.

Movement

We can arrange design elements to draw our eyes around the composition, creating a feeling of excitement and aliveness. The textures we choose play a big role in creating movement within a design, and rhythmic parallel lines or forms help achieve that, as in the example shown here. Radial compositions that fan out from a central point have a feeling of movement as well but are more specifically directed.

Pattern

Pattern introduces a feeling of gentle rhythm within the composition, whether that pattern is based on a grid, or a "brick" pattern where the rows shift slightly, or any other repeated organization of shapes. This method might quiet a composition assembled from an assortment of imagery or textures.

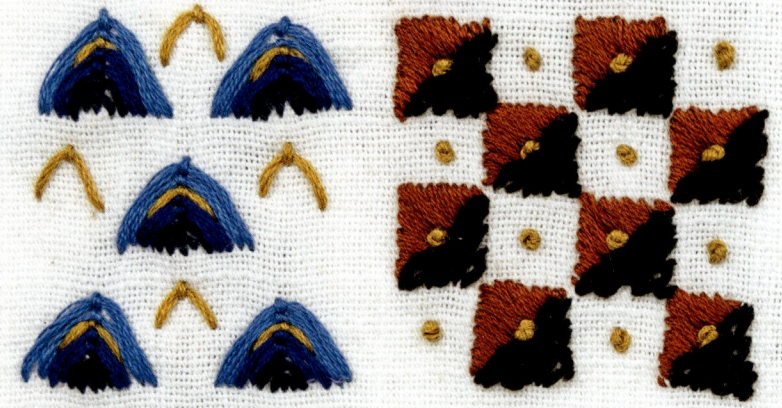

Symmetry

I'm a fan of symmetry, as it gives an immediate feeling of balance and order to a piece. A work that is mirrored—so that the left and right (or top and bottom, or both!) are reflections of each other—is considered symmetrical. Sometimes too much symmetry feels a bit stagnant and expected. Slightly altering the design on the right and left can help. For example, a branch of leaves flanking either side of an object might take up the same space but not be exact replicas of each other. Or, as shown here, the top of the design could be emphasized with stars, while the bottom uses triangles in a similar position and scale.

Bringing asymmetrical arrangements into your composition can create movement, though chaos is an easy pitfall. I sometimes find it helpful to channel the exciting energy of asymmetry into balance by arranging motifs of similar weight on either side of a piece.

Sometimes, as shown in the lower composition, a bit of chaos is exactly what the design needs!

Emphasis

Emphasis creates a central focus, which may not be the literal center. You might emphasize a certain part of the design by having smaller elements point toward the main attraction or frame it. Another strategy is to use more intense color or dramatic textures to emphasize a focal point. If you want a bit of excitement in your artwork, play with asymmetrical compositions that point toward the focus of the piece. If you want to achieve harmony and stability, create radial or symmetrical emphasis.

Proportion

Proportion is basically the scale of elements in relation to each other—how large or small they are. I highly recommend that you roughly sketch different versions of your design to play with proportion. You don't need to detail each element. Draw its basic shape in relation to the other elements, and test out various sizes. Don't always feel like your elements need to fit on the "page" (or hoop, or sleeve, or whatever framed area you plan on filling). Blowing things out of proportion, quite literally, often helps emphasize their importance.

Composing Movement
with Anna Hultin

I begin each embroidered landscape design with a sketch. I map out the basic composition using simple shapes and lines. I rarely sketch color because I'm mainly concerned with how I'm going to use line and shape to create movement within the piece, and the color decisions happen while I'm stitching.

I start each design with a very basic 'middle ground' of texture. From there I look for the things in the landscape that will move the eye around the entire composition. Once I create movement, I add a sky and horizon lines along with any other details. My mind is constantly going between the middle ground, foreground, and background as I'm stitching to make sure that all of them will work together.

I like to try out new materials that will add depth and texture to my work. A few years ago I added roving wool for the first time and the juxtaposition between the thread and the wool created the same juxtapositions of textures I see in a real field."

Anna Hultin's
PRO TIP
My favorite part of any piece is when I feel like it's not working the way I thought it would. This is the point where I can either put down the hoop and give up on it or I can push through. Every time I push through, my work grows in a way I didn't expect.

Designing Compositions

Cut out solid-colored, textured, and shaded shapes from the pages of magazines. The shapes may be geometric, organic, or amorphous—whatever suits your style. Arrange them within a circle or square. Photograph your favorite compositions, print them out, and add them to your sketchbook.

Stitching Compositions

In the ninth position of your sampler, play with the triangular shapes of the fly stitch and feather stitch using balance, movement, pattern, symmetry, emphasis, or proportion to explore composition. Experiment with different lengths, widths, and heights in these stitches, observing how these subtleties affect the way the eye moves around the design.

Plan a grid pattern for the tenth position of your sampler. Fill in the spaces using a stitch of your choice, perhaps trying one you are less familiar with as a way to get to know it better. For example, I used the herringbone stitch here, since I find it challenging to create defined edges with this stitch and I wanted an opportunity to practice.

4
Cultivating Vision

PRACTICES FOR FINDING INSPIRATION, SETTING INTENTIONS, AND STRENGTHENING VISUALIZATION

The rich tradition of infusing expressive meaning into stitches often begins with inspiration, the desire to bring an idea into being. Sometimes, the creative process itself is the source of inspiration. Through experimenting with materials, we may bring forms to life that wouldn't have been born from our minds alone.

From the point of inspiration, we have an opportunity to spell out an intention or goal for our work of art, allowing ourselves to maintain a specific focus. We may have something we'd like to bring to life in our world. We may simply want to decorate our home or wardrobe. Even intentions that seem mundane give us something to work toward.

After we've chosen our intention, we work with the powers of visualization. At the most basic level, we may imagine the finished project in our minds. On a more spiritual level, we may tap into a vision for the future that our force of creativity can help us achieve. Let's look at how these three concepts of inspiration, intention, and visualization work with one another.

Opening to Inspiration

The word *inspiration* stems from the Latin word *inspirare*, meaning "to breathe life into," and is closely related to the word *spiritus*, or breath. To find inspiration is often a two-way street. When we send reverence and awe to an experience, concept, or being, we often meet secrets hidden in its layers. By providing our full attention and focus, we open the door to the potential for breathing in a deeper knowing of what inspires us.

We often want to start projects with a plan, which is our intellect taking the reins. While necessary for tasks like grocery shopping or furniture assembly, starting with intellect might trap us when we want to create new experiences, new imagery, or otherwise innovate. Our intellect gives us what we already know, what we can predict. Art is an opportunity to create what doesn't already exist. Our intuition opens us up to possibility and requires us to loosen up.

When I work on a new piece, much of the design is intuitive. The design flows through me and I ask few questions. As I start to develop this design in more detail, I begin shaping the story. I may adjust the number of corners to improve my overall composition or change that eagle to an owl to better express my idea.

> A combination of intuition and intellect allows new ideas to flow within a bit of structure.

If you steadily record what strikes you in your sketchbook, you will create a well of inspiration. You are drawing this library of imagery from the outer world, through your hands, into your book, and you can pull from it at any time—even many years later—as the perfect addition to the next piece you're working on.

PRACTICES FOR INVITING INSPIRATION

- Get into nature. Sit quietly with a plant or an animal.

- Treat inspiration as a spirit. Make offerings to and meditate on this muse.

- Use limitations. Work in only one color, for example, or only with leftover scraps.

- Read mythologies. Learning about rites, ceremonies, and the creation stories of other cultures opens the mind to seemingly illogical concepts, silencing intellect and carrying our subconscious mind to the dream world.

- Move your body to get out of your head!

Filling the Well
with Tessa Perlow

No matter where you are in your journey as an artist, having a collection of ideas to look back on and draw inspiration from is helpful. I keep lots of sketchbooks with notes, ideas, and drawings. I especially make lots of lists of subject matter and themes I want to work with. If I don't have a solid idea of what I want to do for a piece, I consult my sketchbooks.

My inspiration comes from a lot of different places:

- Walks in my neighborhood or the woods
- Trips to museums and art galleries
- Books and movies
- Researching magic and nature

I'm particularly drawn to:

- Old embroidery samplers
- Surreal art
- Occult art and magic, especially alchemical drawings and the tarot
- Vintage fashions
- Tattoo flash sheets
- Botanical illustrations

Tessa Perlow's
PRO TIP

Keep an inspiration journal. Surrounding yourself with work that you love will inevitably give you ideas for details to bring into your own work or prompt you to consider design choices such as symmetry or asymmetry.

My process is pretty intuitive. I don't spend a long time planning and usually just make a quick sketch of an idea for a garment, hoop, or tapestry. When upcycling clothing, I consider the garment itself—how its seasonality, the texture of the fabric, and the details of construction might influence the design. Then I try to stay open about what direction I take with the work as I stitch, going with the flow of how I'm feeling."

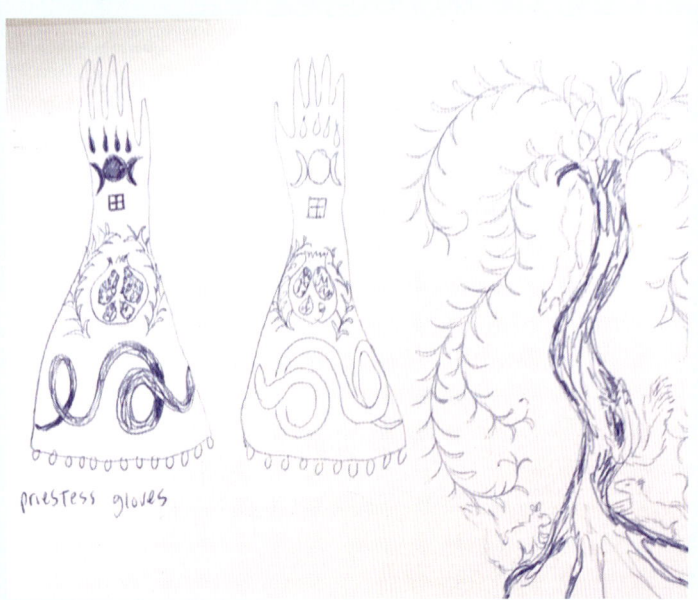

priestess gloves

Knowing Your Intention

An intention might be an aesthetic or practical goal, such as wanting a piece to look good in your home or to cover a stain on a dress. Intention might also be an emotional or transformational goal, such as creating a talisman to support confidence in public speaking, or simply having a good time and quieting the chatter in your own head.

At the very least, working with a grounded intention sharpens the work, ensuring that you only include elements in your design that support the greater vision for your piece and narrowing choices about site or size. More expansively, setting an intention that is specific yet spacious brings clarity to what you desire but keeps you open to the ways in which that desire is fulfilled. That combination of clear focus and flexible receptivity is where the magic of creativity happens!

You can even allow the act of stitching to infuse the fibers with your aspirations—bringing the needle up and down, in and out of the fabric, while imagining the good to come is a way of enchanting cloth with both beauty and the fulfillment of your desires. You may find worries and fears come up during this time. Do not be concerned about stitching these into the fabric. Your embroidery practice is the perfect time to untangle any thoughts standing in the way of what you want to achieve.

This piece is a composite of symbols that remind me of winter nights. My intention was to tune in to the quiet magic that happens in the dark as plants that seem dead get ready for their spring emergence.

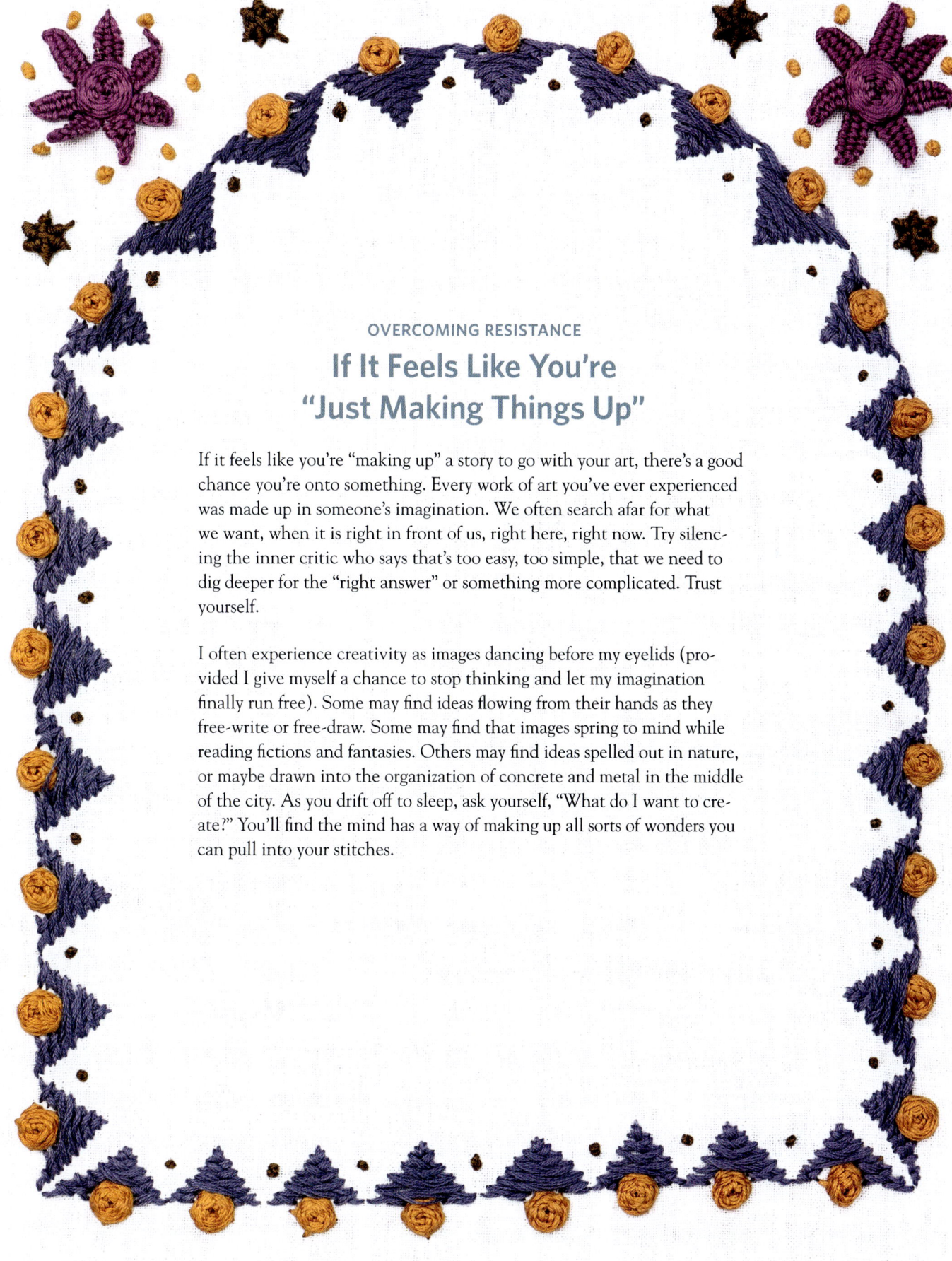

If It Feels Like You're "Just Making Things Up"

If it feels like you're "making up" a story to go with your art, there's a good chance you're onto something. Every work of art you've ever experienced was made up in someone's imagination. We often search afar for what we want, when it is right in front of us, right here, right now. Try silencing the inner critic who says that's too easy, too simple, that we need to dig deeper for the "right answer" or something more complicated. Trust yourself.

I often experience creativity as images dancing before my eyelids (provided I give myself a chance to stop thinking and let my imagination finally run free). Some may find ideas flowing from their hands as they free-write or free-draw. Some may find that images spring to mind while reading fictions and fantasies. Others may find ideas spelled out in nature, or maybe drawn into the organization of concrete and metal in the middle of the city. As you drift off to sleep, ask yourself, "What do I want to create?" You'll find the mind has a way of making up all sorts of wonders you can pull into your stitches.

Accessing Visualization

Visualization is your strongest creative tool, and you use it all the time: when you're hungry and stuck in traffic, and you know exactly what you'd like to eat; or you're bored at work and imagine the sun shining in your eyes, the sand between your toes, on the beach vacation you have planned this weekend. You don't always have to visualize exactly what you wish to create, but having a loose image is often incredibly helpful.

I access visualization by closing my eyes for a few minutes, calming my mind, and throwing out all the to-do lists and random thoughts. Within that state of contemplative consciousness, I envision what does not currently exist. I build images, rebuild them, and try out different styles or compositions, both with the art that I desire to make and with the life I'm trying to live. When we reach *inside* rather than outside ourselves for change or knowledge, the vision is more tangible, and its potential grows greatly.

The beauty of visualization is the way it requires you to focus on exactly what you *do* want to see. We can easily discuss what we don't want, but that gives us very little in the way of moving toward what we do want. I mean sure, we can just say "the opposite of what I don't want," but how boring and vague an image is that?

Practice Remembering Details

To strengthen your visualization muscles if this concept is new to you, or you've had a hard time with it in the past, start with visualizing things you already know exist and can easily re-create in your mind—for example, a lettuce leaf. Close your eyes and see the shades of white and yellow and green, visualize the raised shiny surface, the ruffled edge that's a little darker. The way the stem gets thicker and lighter in color. If you want to move deeper into visualization, involve your other senses, conjuring the distinct smell of lettuce, or hearing the crisp snap of the stem, or imagining the feel of the surface on your hands. Try this with other objects, too. When we practice re-creating images in our mind, we enhance our awareness and tend to spend a little more time looking at the objects that surround us, taking in their subtle hues and precise textures.

Practice Reordering Details

Once you feel comfortable with re-creating what you already know, try using these same techniques for wholly original visions. Try this right now by redesigning the room you're in. First observe the space around you, and after a minute or so, close your eyes and try painting the walls or rearranging the furniture. Maybe tidy up, or even add new windows or doors. Visualization is one of my most effective tools for cleaning or organizing my home! By closing my eyes to see from a distance what that clutter pile is made of and imagining the clutter moving, shifting, and rearranging, I'm able to make better decisions about where everything should be.

Practice Blending and Imagining Details

So how does this apply to creating artwork? I find many folks, me included, try to come up with ideas by looking at a blank page, which is often creatively paralyzing. A blank page provides very little inspiration. But by collecting details of the world around us, we can then start to blend these details together. And for me, this alchemy happens best behind closed eyelids. I'm able to move elements around without needing an eraser, try out new colors without making a single mark, and allow unexpected new images to enter the work.

My visualization process usually starts with a story or a feeling and maybe some simple imagery that feels like it supports my goal. For example, if I want to create a work of art that supports the idea of confidence, I might choose plants, animals, and objects embodying that characteristic: a bear or a lion, a stubborn thistle, or a majestic and deeply rooted oak tree. With my eyes closed, I play with how the forms might take shape, considering compositional elements like balance and emphasis.

If you are struggling, trying to force ideas and connections, or you're not fully content with what is forming, loosen your grip. Clear your mind or shift your pattern of thought. Walk away from your work, make some tea, eat some food, go to bed, and think about it tomorrow.

Have I mentioned that the creative process never enjoys being rushed?

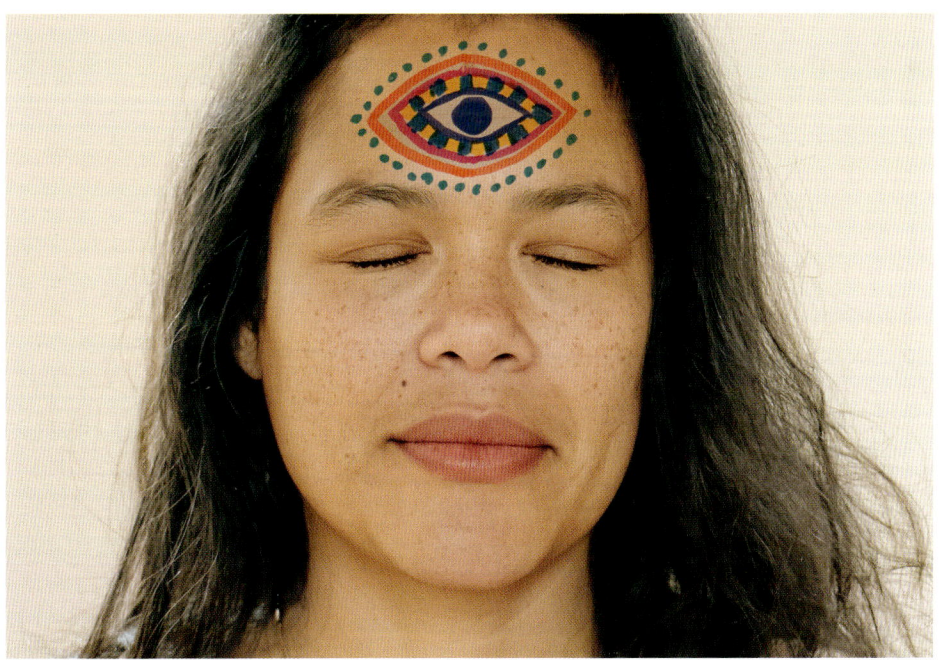

Mining the Psyche
with Valeria Duque

I was never any good at doing things with my hands. I became a photographer so I could be creative using a machine instead. I'm also a perfectionist, and my therapist recommended that I do something just for the fun of it—something I wasn't already good at.

I immediately thought of embroidery and loved it from the first minute, even though I was really bad at first. Once I started embroidering on photographs, I was much better because paper is more rigid than fabric so my stitches look neat and polished.

As with everything handmade, embroidering on paper has been trial and error. From finding paper that is not too flimsy or linty but not too thick to sourcing punching tools suitable for different thread weights, I've had a great time in the process and detached myself from the results.

In my embroidery practice, I like to explore deep aspects of the psyche and unconscious mind, conveying sensations and feelings while reflecting on topics such as gender, self-knowledge, colonialism, beauty, and nature. Embroidery has allowed me to take photography beyond its intrinsic nature of conveying what is actually there. With stitches, I can add textures and patterns that would be impossible to create in real life, helping me to evoke visions, dreams, and intutions."

Valeria Duque's
PRO TIP
When embroidering on paper, the design has to be totally planned in advance. Once you punch a stitch, there's no going back. I use a wide array of punching tools that I've made or found in places such as flea markets and dentists' offices. Whenever possible, I punch one hole at a time to avoid weakening and tearing the paper.

Summoning Vision

Sometimes our experiences seem so mundane that we can't see the greater story in them. Take an element of your personal desire and try to blow it up to mythological proportions. Allow metaphors to run wild and illustrate your desired transformations (or write the story as though it were a fairy tale) in your sketchbook.

* Instead of ruminating on annoying feelings of self-doubt, put on your armor and slay the dragon! What do the scales of this doubt-dragon look like, and what tools do you use in your defense?
* Feeling like you're in a bit of a rut? Climb the rock walls of this rut or build a ladder out of the debris you uncover in this deep crevice.

Not feeling inspired by your own life? Choose a book at random (blindly, or the first one you feel drawn to). Any book will do, but the more fantastical the better. Holding an intention to find vision, flip the book open to a random page or whatever page you are drawn to, and consider how the words and images on the page might serve as guidance. In your sketchbook, draw or write whatever comes up, no matter how seemingly unrelated or uninteresting. This exercise may one day serve as a key to unlock a future mystery.

Stitching Vision

Play with dimensional woven stitches, such as woven picots (page 174), woven wheels (page 176), and spider wheels (page 177). What do their shapes remind you of? In the eleventh position of your sampler, pick two or three of these stitches and explore their textures without a plan.

Visualize what you might create with these stitches. In the twelfth position, experiment with designing a motif or organized arrangement of the stitches. Take a look at your two versions. How does a random approach influence the design compared to a planned approach?

5
Putting It All Together

SAMPLE PROJECTS FOR PERSONAL EXPRESSION

Now you will create a one-of-a-kind piece of art made of your deepest desires! Let's jump-start your creativity with a few practical examples. We'll look at my inspiration for choosing imagery, how I planned my colors, and why I chose specific stitches.

We'll then work with four templates to use as springboards: talismans for abundance, mental clarity, personal transformation, and channeling love. Each will include prompts for visualization to guide your creative process. Think of these templates more like a salad recipe than a baking recipe.

Switch out ingredients freely, borrowing some elements and including your own freshly grown ideas; they do not need to be followed precisely. The basic framework of each provides enough room for personal inspiration to make it distinctly your own design and fulfill your unique objective.

A Blissful Nest

I created this piece as a talisman for cultivating a happy home. The pages of illuminated manuscripts and illustrations of alchemy from the sixteenth and seventeenth centuries inspired my initial sketches. To bring the concepts of alchemical transformation into the realm of the domestic space, I looked to the daily acts of tending a garden and caring for animals as a sort of alchemy for the soul.

Supporting Images: I borrowed elements from my home and garden that bring me joy, and edited them. Climbing hollyhock flowers and crawling aster blossoms flank a large, open doorway that rises from a pedestal decorated with rhythmic patterns. Rudbeckia blossoms and a glowing sun crown the composition. Instead of trying to fit in the whole garden, I picked a few plants that seem to thrive no matter what hardships they face—all the blooms represented are perennials that fight back frost and deer grazing, continuing to set their seed farther each year. The tiger and peacock represent my cat and chickens at a grandiose scale, imparting a fairy-tale energy to the final work.

Supporting Colors: I went a little "more is more" on this one, with as many shades of purples and yellows or golds as I could find, while allowing for turquoise and poppy red to be the bright points of contrast. These bright, vibrant colors felt evocative of an overflowing garden in harvest season, my favorite time of year. Greens in more muted shades allow for moments of quiet in the overall piece.

Supporting Stitches: Because of ample negative space and limited areas to cover, this piece became an opportunity to experiment with different ways of filling with solid color. I practiced stitches such as herringbone (flower petals at the top; the frame of the door), long and short satin stitch (hollyhock blossoms; tiger), and Roumanian couching stitch (triangles on the stairs). With a textural focus on solid fills, I had space to play with maximizing color in this design. Concentrating textured areas on the bottom of the composition grounds the image.

Blooming in the Sky

With this piece, I wanted to illustrate the feeling of divine connection accessed through gardening. *As above, so below* is a common phrase in mystical teachings and can have two meanings: both that our material plane is a reflection of the cosmic plane and that our inner worlds reflect our outer worlds. Tapping into the expansive growth of plants connects us to the expansive growth opportunities of the cosmic realms, and is reflected within our hearts as well. I also wanted to play with a new type of embroidery thread—a thicker matte cotton from DMC—using variations on the chain stitch for the plant, and classic satin stitches for the snake and eye.

Supporting Images: The snake serves as a symbol of transformation (shedding its skin regularly) and dualism (living belowground and spending its days basking in the sun). Awareness of such potential is important in both gardening and life. The large cosmic eye is flanked by leaves arranged in a winglike manner, as though the eye is a rising bird. Below are rudbeckia flowers, which tend to appear in my work often, and the stars hint at a cosmic influence.

Supporting Colors: A black background allows the shades of yellow and green to visually pop, while the rich gold of the snake gives a feeling of warmth, balanced by cool greens on the bottom that help to blend the flowers into the background. I wanted the upper leaves and the lower leaves to read as different realms, so I chose a muted blue-green below and an olive green above. I would usually avoid that color combination, but it seemed to work quite nicely when spaced out by shades of gold and brown.

Supporting Stitches: The thicker threads of the flowers on the bottom become even more dimensional by the choice of detached chain stitches for the petals and fly stitches for the leaves. Stem stitch for the stems always gives a nice flow, but I especially love how it tapers at the end, allowing the stems to blend easily into the background. I used thinner embroidery floss on the eye and leaves up top. That change in the dimension of the thread reinforces the concept of a different realm.

Finding Your Voice
with Ciara LeRoy

I think the best way to create original work is to truly be in touch with yourself and why you are the way you are—you need to understand your own identity. When you're starting out, it's tempting to try to emulate artists and popular styles you admire. There is definitely a place for inspiration, but it's key to pair that inspiration with what is personal to *you* and your lived experience.

Early on in my exploration of embroidery, I embroidered three words together—'RESIST, PERSIST, INSIST.' Those three words capture what I hope to express really well. Much of my work is connected to activism, which requires sometimes heroic amounts of resistance, persistence, and insistence on a better way and world. Those three words also express the fortitude needed to maintain your mental health, sense of identity, and connection to joy—which are other key themes I explore quite often in my artwork.

Since I often incorporate words and lettering into my pieces, embroidery gives me the opportunity to sit with those words for a while—hand embroidery is time consuming, and I often spend that time meditating on the words I'm stitching."

Ciara LeRoy's
PRO TIP
For inspiration, pull from core memories, family history and photo albums, pieces of pop culture that were integral to your upbringing, current events that strike you—anything that connects to your identity or personal calling.

Creating Your Own Talisman

We all have the capacity to create change in our lives. The art of embroidery, with its ups and downs, becomes the perfect practice to meditate on the themes that keep us stuck, bringing them up to the surface so we may thank them and move on with our lives.

You have the power to stitch a vision of the world that you want to see. If one of the themes in the templates I am providing calls to you, let your inspiration blossom within that framework. If an idea of your own has bubbled to the surface and you feel ready, then carve your own path. Either way, go forth and create!

Planning Your Stitches

Whether you choose to design within the templates I'm providing or explore your own themes, let's start by setting an intention and choosing supporting imagery. Our first idea is not always our best. Spend some time making four or five rough drafts, sketching the imagery and design elements in different arrangements. This extra time may help us move past some mediocre designs, while potentially informing future designs. As you sketch, consider the following questions:

* Simpler is often better with a highly textural technique like embroidery, especially when you're a beginner. What parts of the design are essential?
* How might you use differences in scale to add dynamic energy to the design?
* Consider stitch options. Which forms will you define with line, texture, solid spaces, or a combination?
* How much time do you want to spend on the piece? If some of the motifs are quite large, do you want to invest many hours embroidering solid fills, or would it be better to choose an open texture or outline instead?
* If you want areas of solid fill, will you choose a satin stitch for smoothness, stripes of chain stitch for roughness, rows of stem stitch for fluidity, or tightly spaced running stitches or French knots for energy? How might various stitch textures help support the mood of the design you're working on or add visual interest?
* Think about how you'd like the viewer's eye to travel around this piece. What is the movement of energy? How might your choice of stitches or the direction of the stitches help movement not only within the composition but also particular motifs?

I suggest you trace over your final line drawing, either with another sheet of paper, tracing paper, or even the "markup" tool on your phone or any other drawing app. *Draw in your intended stitch textures.* Simulate your seed stitch and your lines of chain stitch, for example. Spending an extra 10 minutes on this step might save you from having to rip out stitches! Get in touch with the overall impact of your drawing by squinting your eyes a little when you look at it. This will help you quickly see what is or isn't working, what needs more or less weight in the composition.

Decision Fatigue

If making decisions about line, texture, color, and composition all at once feels intimidating, consider creating a design using just one color and explore texture and line within your composition. Or maybe choose a single stitch texture instead to focus your exploration on color.

If you find yourself suffering from "analysis paralysis," where your thoughts stop you from even starting, begin making marks. Any marks. They don't have to be good marks. The point is to get your hand-eye coordination moving.

Still confused? Get quiet. Move your body. Get away from the page. Look at it tomorrow. Think about it as you drift off to sleep—the time when I have my best ideas, so I keep a notebook by my bedside. Don't force ideas. No one likes being bossed around!

IT'S A JOURNEY, NOT A DESTINATION

Remember that adjusting and correcting as you go is integral to the creative process. Unpicking stitches, switching out colors, redrawing lines— we take existing information and learn from it. That's not failure. Each creation you make, no matter your opinion of the outcome, informs future creations and increases your capacity to know what you want (and make it happen!).

Garden of Abundance
THE ENERGY OF EARTH

Earth is the home of rich, dark soil that supports and protects many life-forms. There is an opportunity for renewal and nourishment through decomposition of the past. The element of earth is stable and grounding. Work with this energy for calling in fertile ground for growth, prosperity, and a favorable outcome for all.

Writing Prompts

* What do I need in life to feel rooted? How does my body help me understand these needs?

* What areas of my life have crops that are ready to be harvested? How might I bless this bounty and embrace this abundance? How do I continue to feed and nourish myself?

* Is there any rot that I should be composting? Does that sensation live as a deeper knowing in my body? If so, where?

Design Prompts

* Choose one main flower and two secondary flowers to represent abundance. Alternatively, you might choose a single secondary flower that is mirrored on either side of the main one. What flowers evoke an overflowing of riches?

* Choose another plant motif or two to frame the sides of the composition. Are there herbs that support your personal nourishment?

* The central motif is the foundation of this abundance and nourishment. Is there a being or symbol that best represents the stability you require for long-term growth?

* Seven small motifs ground the composition. What other small symbols continue to carry the theme? These might be stars, flowers, bursts of grass blades, or even little bees or butterflies. Alternatively, you might simply choose forms that balance the colors and textures of the rest of the design.

Mental Clarity

THE ENERGY OF AIR

The wind flows past, unable to be captured, as intangible as a thought. Air is the element of intellect, clarity of mind, and perception. Work with this energy to find solutions to a situation or otherwise channel intellectual qualities.

Writing Prompts

* We often have thoughts that arise repeatedly, despite being ineffective. What unanswerable puzzles are you stewing on or overanalyzing? What are your clouds of confusion made of?

* Is there a desired path you feel you've drifted from? How do you see yourself getting back there?

* In what ways does your mind react to new ideas? Do you heed them all the time, push them back until they've been fully processed, or live somewhere between the two?

Design Prompts

* This bird soars above the clouds, seeing with perspective that brings clarity. Its body may symbolize the method for finding your path: a methodical organization of shapes or symbols for those who seek structure, for example, or a single symbol radiating outward for those in need of a clear and specific vision for the future.

* The wings are an opportunity for further symbolism. How will you adorn them with feathers of your own design? Think outside the traditional shape of feathers. Maybe the wings carry herbs of cleansing, or diamonds that help find clarity.

* In the background, continue the poetry of your desires, showing the bird above the clouds or soaring through the stars.

Personal Transformation
THE ENERGY OF FIRE

Ablaze and all-consuming, flames are about forward motion and motivation. The element of fire is transformative and invigorating. Work with this energy to gain strength and stamina or find motivation for change and manifestation.

Writing Prompts

* Visualize a piece of paper or a twig in flames. What do you wish you could burn off rapidly?

* Where are you forcing and pushing that maybe needs more time and care?

* Where in life might you shine brighter?

* Break down your next big move into steps. What does it take to get there?

* Look at the first step. How can you break this down into small actions?

* How will your creation positively influence others around you?

Design Prompts

* Let's decorate the fireplace of our personal transformation! At the base of the hearth, we have a symbol to be offered to the fire. What do you wish to release or sacrifice?

* We flank our offering with herbs to help sweeten the scent. What aromas do you want to associate with your transformation?

* The central fire may burn in any bright color we imagine. What color brings energy to your transformation?

* The tiles or bricks surrounding the fire contain or focus this energy. Triangular shapes might represent direct action. Squares lend an organized sense of stability. Circles might suggest unity.

* The space on top of the mantle is for the symbol of our transformation fulfilled. What will you become?

* Six small elements balance the composition. Will you add more symbols that carry meaning or will these motifs simply enhance the art with color and texture?

Channeling Love
THE ENERGY OF WATER

The realm of the unconscious is deep and fluid. The dreams of our soul reside there as well as general fears we collectively feel. Water is the element of intuition and the emotional realms. Work with this energy to search for partnership, to access intuition while making choices that show love for the self, and to connect with inner visions.

Writing Prompts

* When was the last time you felt yourself inexplicably drawn to something or someone? Where did this feeling live in your body?

* When you feel down or disappointed, what are your go-to choices for self-soothing? Is there an activity you can begin to incorporate that may better nourish you?

* What sensitivities have you not given time to feel? How can you welcome these unknown forces within your being?

Design Prompts

* You are now the architect of your own fountain, designing the symbols through which your emotions and love will flow. The base of the fountain is a bowl shape, but that structure could be any vessel in which feelings are stored and from which feelings emerge. Deeply rooted ferns, cradled hands . . . what other images could represent this vessel for holding emotions?

* The middle tier of the fountain filters and blesses the waters as they fall. What creates the bowl shape of this container? An opening blossom, an ornate chalice, or some other sign of good fortune?

* The top tier of the fountain contains space for a symbol that focuses and centers what emotion you would like to emerge. A mushroom might suggest the mycelial network of connection. To symbolize belonging, a fish might be appropriate within the water theme. What supporting image will crown your fountain?

* At the top of the composition, there is space for a symbol that represents a higher spirit to watch the movement of the fountain and guide you. What is looking after your fountain?

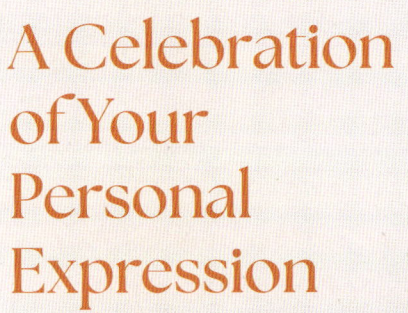

A Celebration of Your Personal Expression

You made it to the end of the workshop—hooray! No matter the results of your sampler, or the look of your sketchbook pages, if you've practiced even a fraction of the experiments in this book, give yourself a pat on the back. You have carved out time for yourself and expanded your ideas of what's possible, hopefully both in your stitching and in your life. (Creativity tends to trickle out and affect us in unexpected ways.) May this book continue to inspire you on your artistic journey.

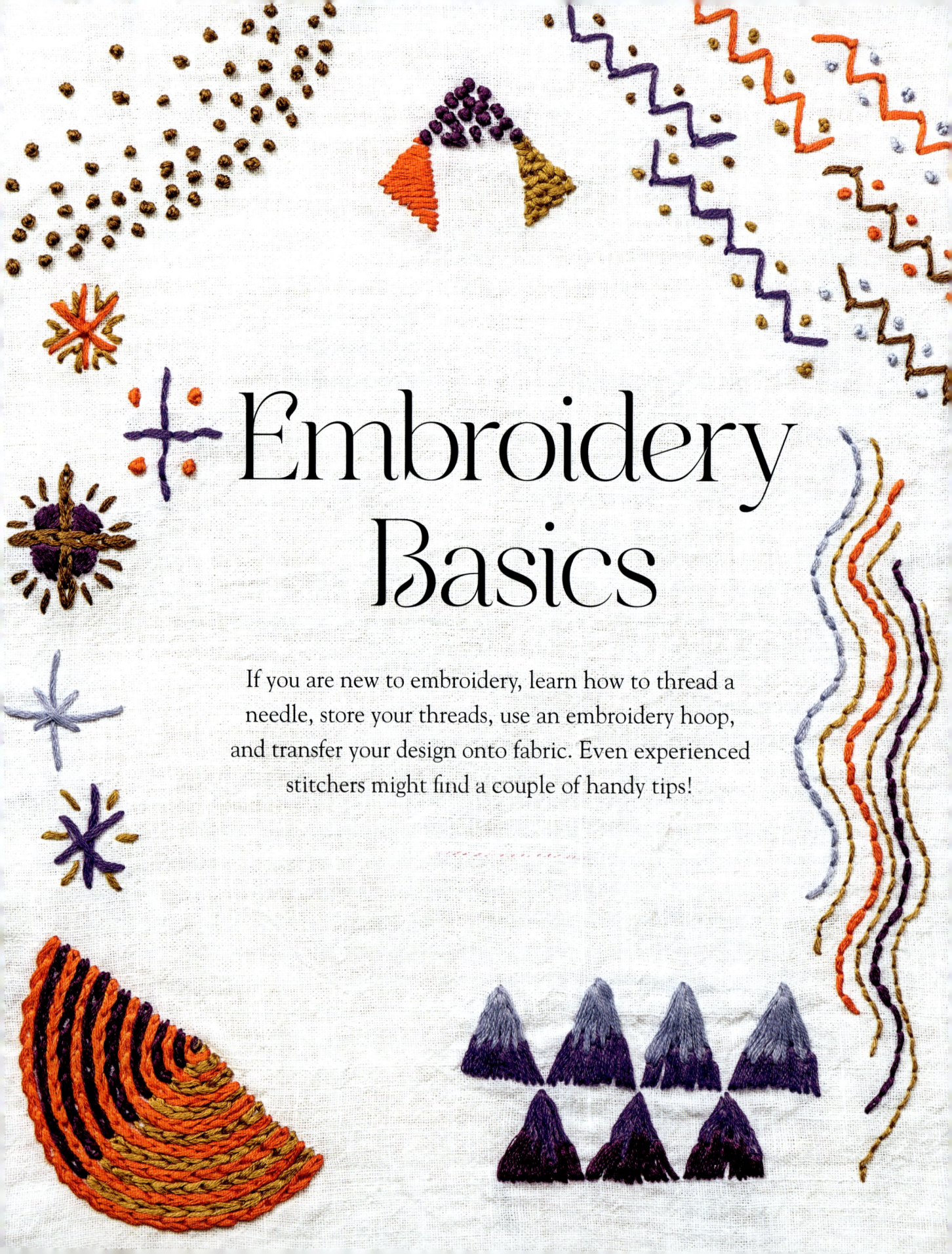

Embroidery Basics

If you are new to embroidery, learn how to thread a needle, store your threads, use an embroidery hoop, and transfer your design onto fabric. Even experienced stitchers might find a couple of handy tips!

How to Thread a Needle

Begin with a piece of embroidery thread at a length that is comfortable for stitching. An easy way to measure this is from one shoulder to the other hand, stretching out to the side. This stretch is like the motion you make when stitching. Threads longer than this may get tangled.

Threading the needle is easiest when you've cut the thread cleanly with *sharp* scissors. Licking the end of the thread helps immensely. This is the method for threading that has worked well for me:

* Pinch the end of the thread between the thumb and forefinger of your nondominant hand. Holding the needle in your dominant hand, place the eye of the needle over the pinched thread.

* Slowly roll the tips of your fingers outward to expose more of the thread, pushing the needle down into the end, giving the thread nowhere to go but into the eye of the needle.

A needle threader is a cheap and useful addition to your toolbox. Skip the ones made of thin wire that breaks easily, and try one made of thin, flat metal with a large hook on one end and a small hook on the other. LoRan is my favorite brand. Insert the hook in the eye of the needle, loop the thread around the hook, and pull through.

Double knot at one end and pull the needle from the back of the fabric to the front so the knot stays hidden at the back.

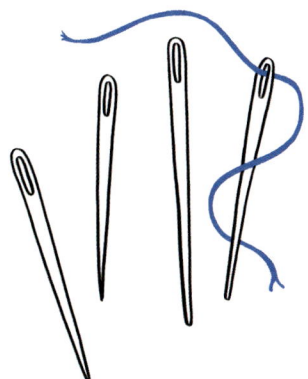

How to Store Threads

You can wind threads on bobbins to prevent tangling, but I usually keep them in their packaging. Pulling the thread from the barcode end of a DMC skein also prevents tangles. Save leftover pieces by wrapping the thread around your thumb and forefinger in a figure eight. With the last few inches, wrap the middle of this bundle and tie. To use, pull from the loose end of the bundle.

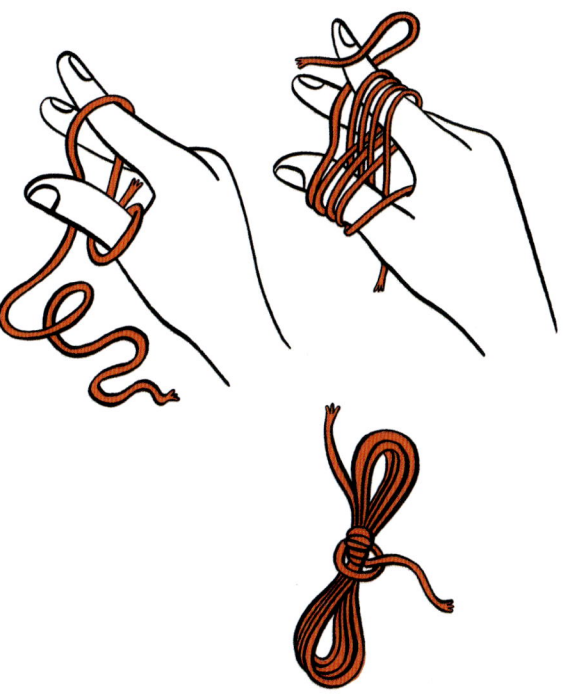

How to Use an Embroidery Hoop

The traditional style of embroidery hoop is composed of two parts: the outer hoop, which has a small screw, and the inner hoop, which is a continuous piece. The screw on the outer hoop is used for adjusting the tightness. I use wood or bamboo hoops. There are two ways to set up your hoop. One is for transferring designs onto the fabric and the other is for stitching. For both setups, start with the adjustable hoop slightly loose, so you can reposition the fabric a bit if necessary.

To use a hoop for embroidery: Place the fabric right side up over the small continuous hoop, then place the adjustable hoop over the fabric and other hoop.

Once you have your fabric sandwiched between the two hoops, tighten the adjustable hoop just enough so you can pull the fabric taut on all sides. Take care to pull with the grains of the fabric so the weave doesn't distort. You should be able to see the grid of the weave running straight up and down and straight back and forth like graph paper. When it's all set up, tighten the screw again and gently pull your fabric taut like a drumhead, keeping the weave straight. As you embroider, you may need to adjust the tension, as it naturally loosens while you work.

The size of the hoop you use depends on the size of the work. I use 4" hoops for tiny designs on small areas like sleeves, 6" hoops for general work, and 8" hoops for oversized designs. If the design is bigger than 8", move the hoop around the work, stitching one segment at a time. Don't worry about flattening previously embroidered stitches with the hoop. They'll fluff back up when you remove the hoop.

To use a hoop for framing: To frame your embroidery in your hoop once you're done stitching, trim excess fabric, leaving a 1" edge all around. Glue the edges to the back, inside of the hoop, or gather them on the backside of the piece and secure them with a large running stitch.

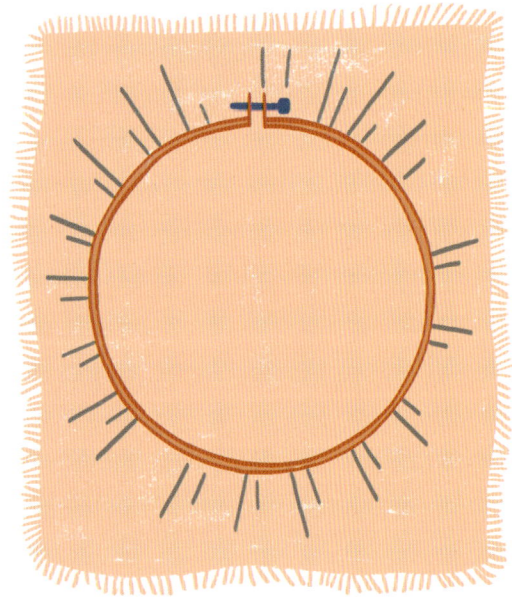

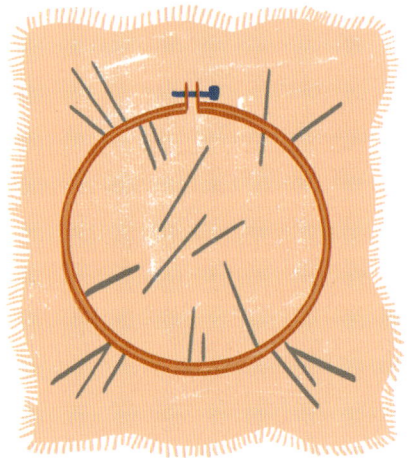

How to Transfer a Design to Fabric

There are many methods and tools available to transfer the outlines of your final sketch to fabric. I find the light-box method to be most convenient and effective. If the fabric is darker or thicker, the transfer paper method might be better.

Light-Box Method

Use an actual light box or a window on a bright day. Work with a marking tool that will disappear (see box below).

Start by taping your sketch onto the glass. Then place the fabric faceup over the paper. Be sure to center the fabric properly. Keep the fabric in the same place, taping it down on four sides if needed.

With the light coming through the back of the glass, you should be able to see the sketch through the fabric. Carefully trace the design onto the fabric with your marking tool of choice.

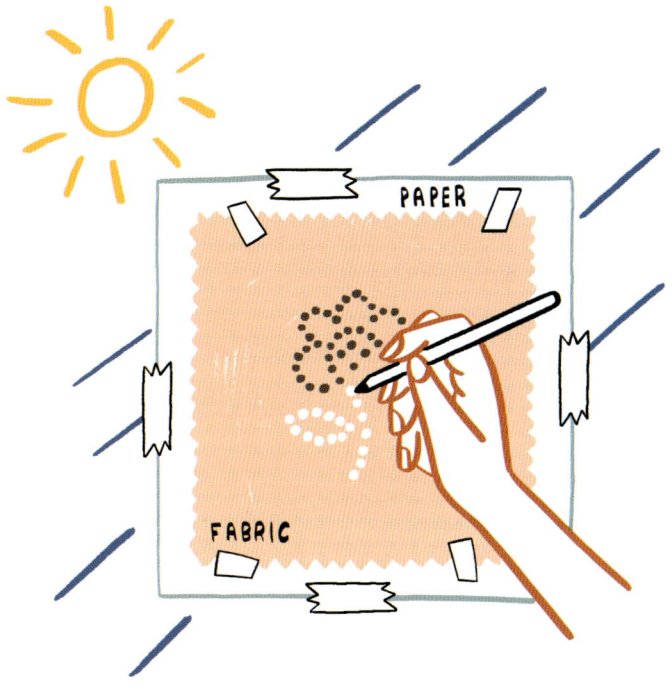

MARKING TOOLS

I love Caran d'Ache watercolor pencils in white or ivory because they are not waxy like Prismacolor or other colored pencils and will wash out. Do not use a darker color of Caran d'Ache pencils because they could bleed and not wash out.

Crayola Ultra Clean Washable Markers come in many colors, and I have never had a problem with them leaving a permanent mark, though I recommend testing any markers or pencils on a swatch of your fabric.

I also love Pilot FriXion heat erasable rollerball pens. To remove the ink, use a hair dryer or gently iron the back of the embroidery (not too hard—you don't want to smash your stitches). White heat-erase gel pens are a valuable tool for working with dark fabrics, and you'll find them at most sewing supply stores. I find that heat-erase pens, especially the white gel pens, are most permanently removed with washing. If you wear a garment in temperatures below freezing, the ink could reappear.

There are other brands of washable and air-erase markers that are designed to wash out or fade over time. They are fine for many applications, though I find they sometimes air-erase before I'm done stitching; in humid areas this may happen in just a few hours. They also do not seem to wash out of naturally dyed fabrics. You've been warned! Testing first is the best policy!

Transfer Paper Method

The transfer paper method is a good option if you are using fabric that is too dark or thick to work with a light box. Saral transfer paper comes in an affordable sampler pack of five colors, washes out, transfers nicely onto fabric, is reusable, and is available at many different types of stores.

You'll need a hard, smooth surface to get a sharp line, so place the fabric faceup on a table. Sandwich the transfer paper, chalk side down, between the fabric and your sketch. Be sure to center the design properly. To keep the paper in the same spot, tape it onto the fabric.

Use a dull-tip pencil, the back end of a small paintbrush, or another instrument to trace the design. Be careful not to tear the paper. After transferring the design, use a marking tool to go over the lines again. Transfer paper chalk sometimes doesn't last for the entirety of your embroidery project.

PRINTABLE TRANSFER PAPER

There are also a variety of embroidery transfer papers that can go through the printer or photocopier, then iron or stick onto the fabric. These are a great option if you do not feel confident in your tracing skills. Sulky and Pellon are two brands that offer a variety of these papers. Look for options that indicate that they stick to fabric. I also love Printworks Vanishing Fabric Transfers and DMC Magic Paper.

Stitching Basics

Stitching almost always begins in the same way—by knotting the thread and pulling the thread through from back to front so the knot on the back of the fabric holds the thread securely. Bring the tip of the needle up at the beginning of your line of stitching.

Try to keep your stitches a little loose. If your fabric is puckering, your stitches are too tight. You don't need to pull until the thread is tight—just pull until the thread lies flat on the fabric. A little slack is fine and will ensure the final piece of work doesn't warp the fabric and create wrinkles. Also, cotton threads often shrink a tiny bit in the wash. If you're embroidering on clothing that will end up being laundered, be sure to leave a little slack in your stitches. I've never in all my workshops seen a student create stitches that were too loose.

When working on curved lines, you may have to use a smaller stitch. Imagine connecting dots to create a line. If you have a sharp curve, a long stitch will make it look more like a corner, while a bunch of tiny stitches gives a more fluid effect.

Stitch Methods

These foundational stitches provide you with a beautiful range of textures and weights to play with in your designs. Expand the range of effects even more by experimenting with stitch length and thread weight.

Backstitch, see p. 164

Running Stitch, see p. 165

Ray Stitch, see p. 165

Seed Stitch, see p. 165

Stem Stitch, see p. 166

Star Stitch, see p. 167

Split Stitch, see p. 166

Cable Stitch, see p. 168

Satin Stitch, see p. 168

Long and Short Stitch, see p. 169

Herringbone Stitches,
see pp. 171–72

Roumanian Couching Stitch,
see p. 169

Bokhara Couching Stitch, see p. 170

Cretan Stitches, see pp. 170–71

French Knot, see p. 173

Couching, see p. 176

Woven Wheel, see p. 176

Bullion Stitch, see p. 173

Grid Stitch, see p. 175

Woven Picots (attached needle weaving), see p. 175

Spider Wheel, see p. 177

Woven Picots (detached picot), see p. 174

Wrapped Stitch, see p. 178

Chain Stitches, see pp. 181–82

Fly Stitch, see p. 183

Double Chain Stitch, see p. 184

Magic Chain Stitch, see p. 184

Blanket Stitches, see pp. 178–80

Feather Stitch, see p. 185

Backstitch

This classic continuous stitch is used for outlines and fine details, and closely resembles a sewing machine stitch. For fine detail work, use shorter-length stitches of ⅛ inch and split the embroidery floss down to two or three strands.

1. After bringing the needle up at the beginning of the line, insert the needle back into the fabric a little less than ¼ inch (or whatever stitch length you've chosen) from where the thread came out.

2. Bring the needle back out this same distance ahead, and pull the thread through until taut.

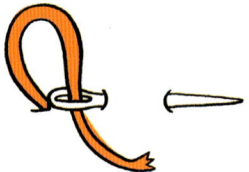

3. Insert the needle back into the closest end of this first stitch.

4. Bring the needle out one stitch length ahead of where the thread just came out.

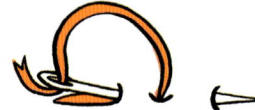

5. Continue inserting the needle into the end of the previous stitch.

6. Continue exiting one stitch length ahead to create a solid, continuous line.

Running Stitch

Created by simply running in and out of the fabric with the needle, this stitch can be made in a variety of ways for different results. You can create an even stitch length so the part of the thread that goes under the fabric is the same length as the part that is seen above. Or you can choose to make longer stitches on top, only picking up a tiny bit of fabric between stitches. Or you can create tiny stitches on the top of the fabric while the needle goes behind the fabric for larger gaps between stitches. When making curved lines with the running stitch, you may need to use smaller stitches and pick up fewer stitches at a time. Keep the running stitches under ⅜ inch to prevent snagging on wearable items.

1. Bring the thread to the surface. Insert the needle back into the fabric at the desired distance of the stitches on the surface.

2. Bring the needle back out along the stitch line.

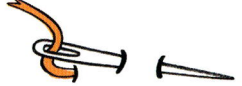

3. Continue this in-and-out motion; once you get the hang of it, you can create multiple running stitches in the same motion before pulling the thread through.

Ray Stitch

The ray stitch is another type of running stitch. To create expanding rays, bring the needle to the surface at the top of the first ray, then back into the fabric at the bottom of the ray. Running the needle under the fabric diagonally, bring it out again at the top of the second ray and then back at the bottom of that ray. Continue until the last ray is complete.

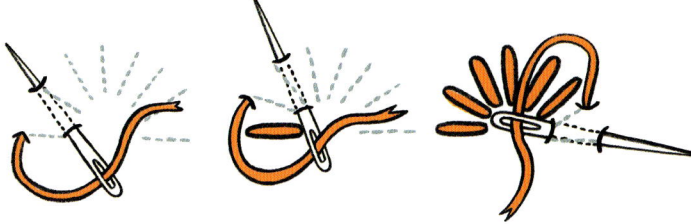

Seed Stitch

This texture is created by making random running stitches and is usually used to fill in areas. There are many options for this technique. You can stitch them close together for an opaque effect. You can overlap the stitches for full coverage. Or you can vary the distance or size of the stitch to create shading. This method works best when the chaos of stitches on the back is hidden, so use an opaque fabric. This is one of those challenges where you're required to be consistently inconsistent. It may take some practice to get the hang of it. Think of it like sprinkles on a cupcake, or pickup sticks. They all scatter about in different directions, creating an exciting pattern of chaos.

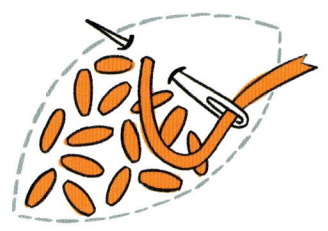

Split Stitch

This smooth and fluid line is created by "splitting" the previous stitch. Parallel rows of split stitch can be used as a filling. As with the backstitch, be sure to make shorter stitches when creating tight curves with the split stitch.

1. Bring the needle up at the beginning of the line. Insert the needle into the fabric one stitch length ahead (about ¼ inch, or shorter for details and curved lines).

2. Pull the thread through all the way to the back until the stitch lies flat.

3. Bring the needle up in the middle of this first stitch, piercing through and "splitting" the thread.

4. Insert the needle back into the fabric ¼ inch from this point and pull to the back.

5. Repeat, each time splitting up through the previous stitch.

Stem Stitch

To create this ropelike effect, you'll be making stitches slightly offset from one another. Be sure that the needle is coming out of the same side on every stitch for a consistent look. As you work, the tip of the needle should be facing your previous stitches. For tight curves and details, keep this stitch very short, ⅛ inch or so.

1. After bringing the needle out of the fabric at the beginning of the line of stitching, insert the needle ¼ to ⅜ inch along the line. The dots in the illustration indicate where the needle will come in and out of the fabric. It may also help to learn this stitch by marking the fabric with dots spaced ¼ inch apart.

2. With the needle facing the direction you started, bring the needle back out at the halfway mark between where the thread came out and where the needle went in.

3. Now insert the needle one stitch length ahead; the end of the previous stitch will line up with the middle of this new stitch.

4. Bring the needle out at the end of the last stitch.

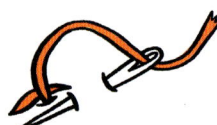

5. Continue along the stitch line marked, making sure each stitch is the same length.

THE S AND Z RULE

When creating a piece of work with multiple stem stitches, it will look best if the stitches are going at the same angle. The best way to remember this is the S and Z rule: Is the angle of your previous stitches creating the angle of the letter S or the letter Z?

Star Stitch

This is a simple way to create celestial stars composed of three straight stitches overlapping and one stitch holding them down in the middle. The order of the three stitches that make the star is not important, but it helps to mark them out first so the spacing is right.

1. Start by marking six dots for the points of your star. It helps to visualize how they will connect, but you don't need to draw the dotted lines connecting the points.

2. Bring the thread up at one end of a ray. Insert the tip of the needle into the point on the opposite side. Either pull the thread to the back and come up at the next point, or take a shortcut by inserting the tip of the needle in the next point before pulling through the thread. This will bring you back on top and ready to stitch the next ray.

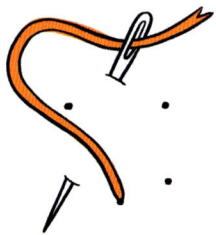

3-4. Repeat step 2 with the remaining rays, overlapping them in the middle.

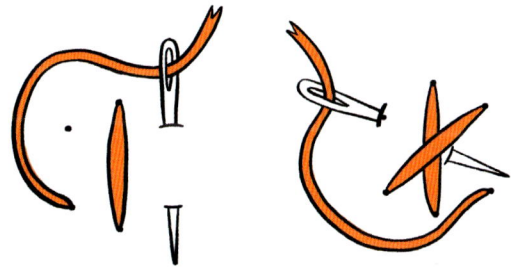

5. Bring the tip of the needle up at one side of the overlapped center. Tack down these three stitches by inserting the needle into the other side of the intersection, and pull the thread flat.

Cable Stitch

Used in rows, the cable stitch creates a bricklike effect with a lovely texture. It's also ideal for filling areas with bulky threads that are too bold for satin stitch (at right). Create the cable stitch by making two rows of stitching at once: one on top and one on the bottom, alternating rows as you stitch.

1. **Top row of stitching:** After bringing the needle up at the beginning of the line, insert the needle into the fabric one stitch length ahead and come out halfway back, one thread width below.

2. **Bottom row of stitching:** Insert the needle one stitch length ahead and come out at the end of the last stitch, one thread width above.

3. Continue inserting the needle one stitch length ahead, bringing the needle out at the end of the last stitch, alternating the angle of the needle so the stitches alternate between top row and bottom row.

Satin Stitch

This works well for covering areas with smooth, uniform stitches. For wearable items, you want to keep the stitches under ½ inch long so they don't snag. The back of this stitch should look the same as the front. Consider the shape you will be filling with this stitch before you start and which direction the stitches should go. The shorter the better!

1. Bring the needle out at one edge and insert it back in at the other edge, pulling through until the stitch is just a little bit raised. If you pull too tight, the tension will cause the fabric to pucker.

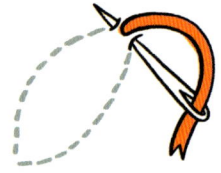

2. Insert the needle as close as possible to the previous stitch.

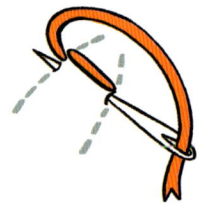

3. Continue, with the needle coming back up as close as possible to the previous stitch. If you're creating a curved shape, like the color arcs in a rainbow, for example, it helps to fill in the gaps on the wider edge of the arc with half stitches. This will help them blend in well visually.

half stitches

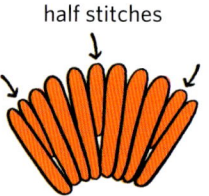

Long and Short Stitch

Use this stitch to shade areas. By blending two or more colors together, you can fill in areas too large for a flat satin stitch in a single color. For example, a solid area that needs stitches longer than 1 inch is likely to get snagged. Instead, fill it in with this stitch while still achieving the beautiful texture of a satin stitch. This is not a stitch that requires perfection. A little randomness to the long and short helps to soften the texture.

1. Begin your stitch on one edge of the area to be shaded, alternating between long and short satin stitches. The stitches should all line up on one edge, and the other edge will be staggered with long and short stitches. As you learn this stitch, it may help to draw lines for each section of color as shown, creating rows about ¼ inch apart with an erasable marker or pencil.

2. On the next row (or in the next color if you're shading areas with multiple colors), split up through the end of the previously created stitches, then insert the needle two rows up. Bring the needle out by splitting up through the next stitch on the previous row. From here on, each stitch will be two "rows" long, which will stagger the edge and create a visual effect of blending the stitches.

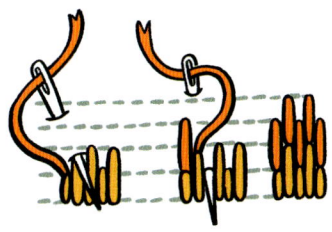

3. Make long stitches of equal length, which will continue the staggered long-and-short effect. Continue this with as many colors as necessary, or as many rows as necessary if you're filling with a solid color.

   If you're aiming for an even edge on the other side of the shaded area, finish with the same one-long, one-short stitches as the first row.

Roumanian Couching Stitch

The Roumanian and Bokhara couching stitches are common in suzani embroideries from Uzbekistan as well as the embroideries of Indian Banjara communities. They are an extension of the satin stitch (see facing page), except instead of a single long stitch on the back and front, you'll bring the thread back up to the surface, making a long diagonal stitch that pins down the original stitch. Due to the doubling of thread in the middle, the long stitches should be slightly more spaced out than you usually would make the satin stitch.

1. Bring the needle out at one edge of the planned design, and insert it back in at the other edge.

2. Bring up the needle about ¼ inch back from the end of this stitch, one thread width below.

Roumanian couching stitch continued on next page

3. Insert the needle into the fabric about ¼ inch ahead of the opposite edge, one thread width above, bringing the needle back out at the original edge, one thread width below. This stitch tacks down the original stitch with a long diagonal crossover.

4. Repeat steps 1 through 3 with parallel lines of stitching.

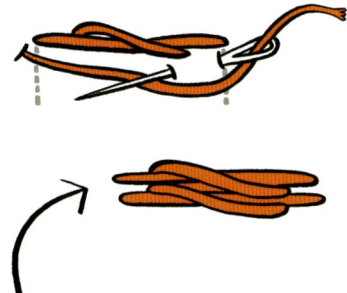

Note that the stitches are a bit spaced out at the ends.

Bokhara Couching Stitch

The Bokhara stitch is similar in concept to the Roumanian stitch, but instead of a longer tack stitch, create short tack stitches at regular intervals along the original stitch. Use the same "come out on the bottom, go in at the top" technique described, just with much shorter diagonal stitches.

Cretan Stitch

Getting its name from the island of Crete in Greece, this stitch is common in Greek embroideries. Textile artists in Mexico and Guatemala also use it to join seams. Begin by drawing four parallel lines equidistant from each other. The rhythm of this stitch is to bring the needle out at a middle line (B or C), in at an edge line (A or D). Repeating this as you stitch might help: "Come out the middle; go in the edge." Drawing a zigzag in the middle (between lines B and C) helps you space your stitches.

1. Start by bringing the needle *out* at line B, *in* at line D, at a diagonal.

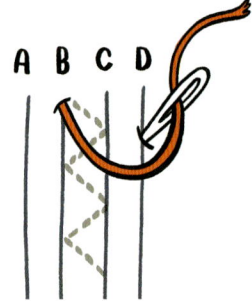

2. Now go *out* at line C, making sure the thread tucks under the tip of the needle. By allowing the thread to dangle down, this will happen naturally as you stitch.

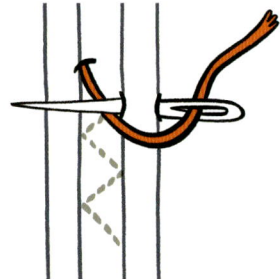

3. Bring the needle *in* at line A, *out* at line B, tucking the thread under the tip of the needle.

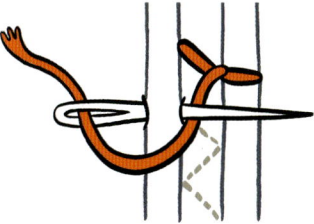

4. Continue this rhythm: in at D, out at C, in at A, out at B.

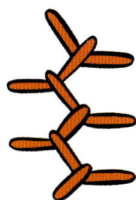

Closed Cretan Stitch

The rhythm is the same, but the stitches are much closer together.

Cretan Leaf

Draw four parallel lines that meet at a point at the top and the bottom, then follow the instructions for the Cretan stitch, making the stitches very close together.

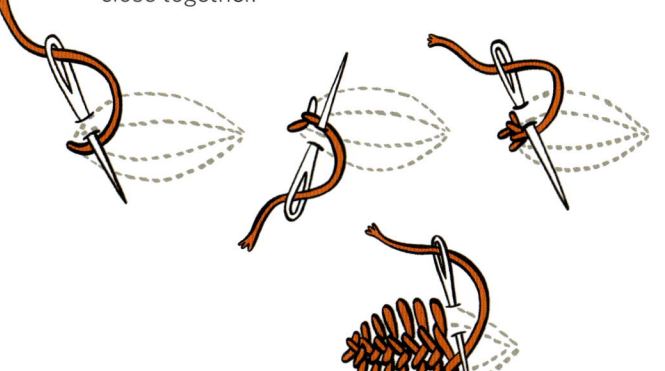

Herringbone Stitch

This fun stitch is common in Mexican Tenango and Indian Banjara embroideries. Play with spacing. Making the stitches closer together gives a denser effect, while changing the angle of the diagonals gives you different options as well. Begin by drawing two parallel lines to mark the top and bottom edges of the stitch.

1. Bring the needle out on the left edge of the lower line. Insert the needle into the upper line a little to the right, creating a diagonal stitch. Then, with the needle facing the beginning of the line, bring its tip out about ⅛ inch away along the top line and pull through.

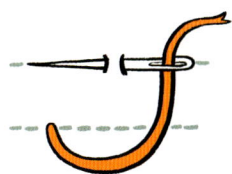

2. Crossing over the first diagonal stitch, insert the needle into the lower line a little to the right, then backstitch about ⅛ inch away on the bottom line and pull through.

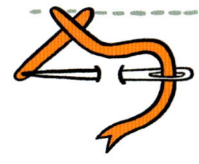

3. Continue crossing over the previous stitch, creating a backstitch on the opposite line until the end.

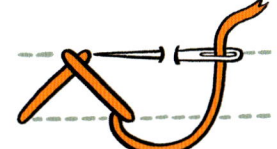 

Closed Herringbone

This is the same motion as the regular herringbone stitch, but the stitches are much closer together. Bring the needle out where the last stitch ended.

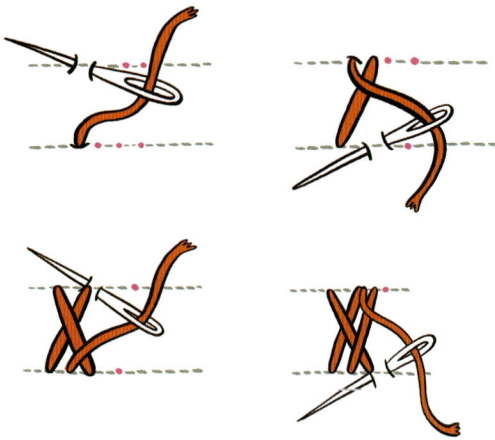

Leaf Herringbone

This stitch is the same as the closed herringbone, but insert the needle in and out on the outer edges of a leaf shape instead of on parallel lines. The first few stitches will be very short and nearly vertical.

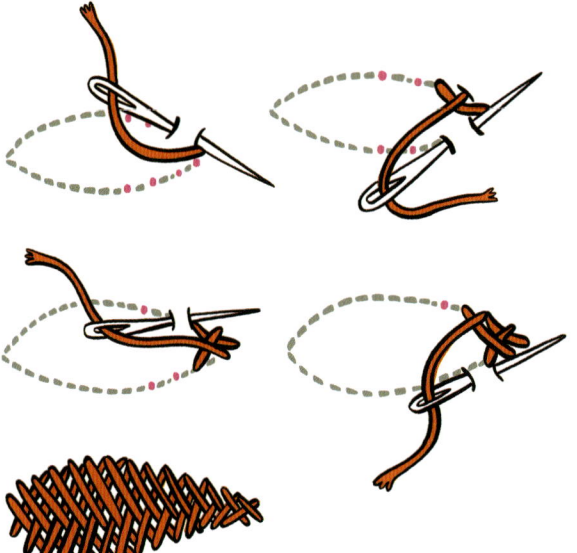

Raised Herringbone

This stitch creates a three-dimensional shape perfect for leaves or droplets.

1. Create a single vertical stitch down the center, halfway from the middle. Bring the needle out at the top.

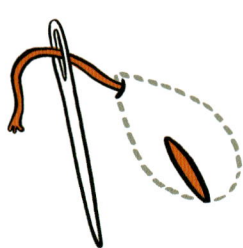

2. Slip the needle under the single vertical stitch.

3. Crossing over the new stitch, insert the needle just to the right of the top of the stitch, bringing it out just to the left of the top of the stitch.

4. Continue slipping the needle under the vertical stitch, and stitching from right to left until you reach the bottom edge of the shape. The more stitches you squeeze onto the leaf, the more raised the effect will be.

5. Pull the thread to the back when the leaf is sufficiently filled in.

French Knot

Use a French knot to create a pretty raised dot in your design. It may take a few tries to get the hang of this stitch. If the knot isn't staying, check that you are wrapping the needle from the eye toward the tip, and that the knot isn't pulling through the fabric to the back. If your knots continue to pull to the back, it may be because your fabric has a very open weave. In that case, try a bigger knot by wrapping the thread around the needle twice.

1. After pulling the thread through to the front, wrap the thread around the needle very closely to the fabric (one wrap makes a small knot, two make a bigger knot), while pulling the loose end of the thread securely.

2. Insert the needle just a tiny bit from where the thread came out of the fabric, then pull through to the back.

3. Gently pull the thread all the way through, holding the knot down with your fingertip to keep it from tangling.

When creating French knots on top of a satin stitch or other filling stitches, you'll want to insert the needle about ⅛ inch from where the thread came out, tacking down an entire width of thread on the satin stitch so the French knot doesn't get lost in the stitches below.

Bullion Stitch

This stitch makes a beautiful textured bump on the surface of the fabric. The more times you wrap the needle, the more raised the bump is. With thick threads, even wool tapestry yarns, you can create highly dimensional shapes using this stitch.

1. Start by making a straight stitch the length of the desired bullion, leaving a large loop.

2. Bring the needle out where the stitch began.

3. Wrap the loop of thread around the shaft of the needle as many times as needed to equal the desired bullion length, condensing the spiral snugly but not tightly.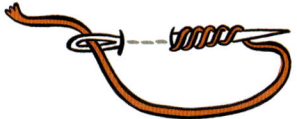

4. Holding the spiral down with your finger, pull the needle through.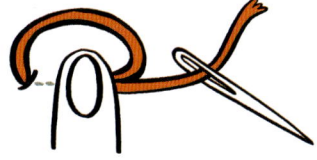

Bullion stitch continued on next page

5. Pull the straight length of thread through the spiral, while pushing on the end of the spiral, until the wrap lies flat against the fabric.

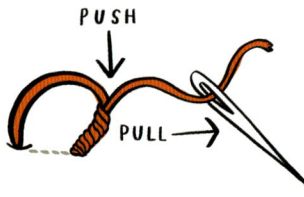

6. Insert the tip of the needle into the end of the stitch and pull to the back.

Depending on how many times you wrap the thread around the needle in step 3, your bullion stich will lie flat against the fabric or create a loop.

Woven Picots

Needle weaving creates three-dimensional shapes that pop off the surface of the embroidery, perfect for petals or leaves. Either leave the tip detached, which creates a twist in the shape, or attach the thread at both ends to better control where the shape ends.

Detached Picot

This technique creates a triangular shape in which only the base of the triangle is attached to the fabric. The tip is loose.

1. Fasten a straight pin into the fabric. Where the pin enters the fabric marks the tip of the triangle; where it exits marks the base. This pin will keep your threads taut while you weave them.

2. Bring the needle out at the bottom left corner of the triangle. Tuck the thread behind the top of the pin from left to right (not going into the fabric, just tucking behind the pin) and bring the needle into the bottom right corner of the triangle. Bring the needle back out at the middle of the bottom edge and pull it through.

3. Tuck the thread behind the top of the pin from left to right again. These three strands are now the warp threads that you will be weaving in and out of.

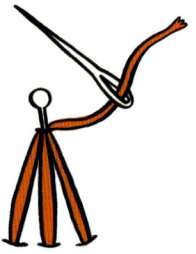

4. Starting at the top where the thread has been tucked behind the pin, begin by weaving the needle under the far-right strand, over the middle strand, and back under the left strand.

5. Come back in the other direction, weaving the needle over the outer strands and under the middle strand.

6. Continue to alternate your weaving rows, repeating steps 4 and 5. Use the needle to push the woven rows up (so they are closer together) every few passes.

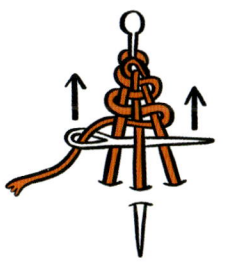

7. When you get to the bottom, insert the needle into the bottom edge at any point and pull the thread to the back. Remove the pin and admire your work!

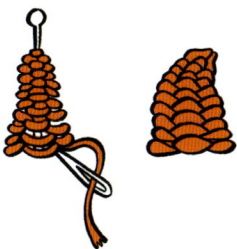

Attached Needle Weaving

Attached on both ends, this technique creates a woven band.

1. Create three or more stitches in any arrangement, such as parallel lines for a rectangle or radiating lines for a triangle. These stitches are the warp threads that you weave through. For a more three-dimensional shape, make these initial warp stitches a bit loose, allowing the woven stitches to rise off the fabric.

2. Bring the needle out at one end and begin weaving through your warp threads, alternating over and under.

Grid Stitch

To fill in an area, create a square grid using straight stitches. Tack down each intersection with a single stitch (shown at the top of the illustration), making sure all tack stitches are going in the same direction. For a more pronounced effect, tack each intersection down with crossing stitches (shown on the left).

Couching

Couching works well as an outline and requires two threads: a thicker, possibly more decorative one that lies along the surface (surface thread), and a thinner one to stitch the surface thread down (stitching thread). Either match the color of the surface and stitching threads or use different colors to play with contrast. For a deeply dimensional effect, try bundling multiple strands of embroidery thread or using heavier string, cord, or yarn for your surface thread. Knitted jersey fabric naturally rolls into a cord when cut into thin strips. Take advantage of this!

1. Mark your outline on fabric. Begin by knotting your surface thread and pulling it through from the back with a large-eyed tapestry or upholstery needle. If the thread or other material is too thick to pull through fabric, stitch the end down securely with a matching sewing thread.

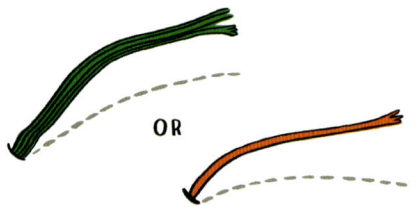

2. Lay the surface thread along the outline. With a second smaller needle, bring the stitching thread up through the fabric on one side of the surface thread. Cross the surface thread, creating a small stitch perpendicular to the outline.

3. Continue stitching down the surface thread. Each stitch should come out of and go into the outline, so the stitches appear to be tucking underneath the surface thread. These may be as close together as possible or up to ½ inch apart, depending on the curve of the line. Sharper curves require closer stitches.

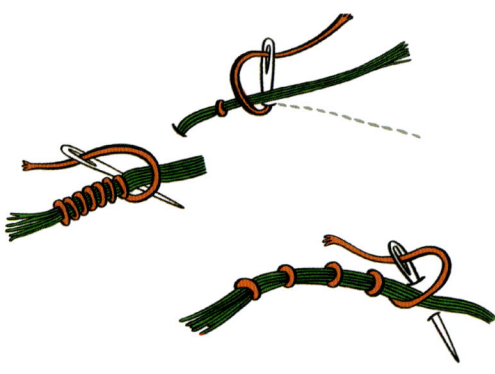

Woven Wheel

This technique creates a circular shape with many possible variations and uses. Weaving only a few rows, while allowing the spokes to remain exposed, results in a star shape. Weaving loosely around the full length of the spokes results in a textured circle. Continuing to weave a few extra rows after the shape is filled raises the wheel to resemble a three-dimensional flower.

1. Mark the outline of a circle on your fabric. Stitch an odd number of evenly spaced spokes. With each spoke, bring the needle up at the edge of the outline and down in the center of the circle.

2. After creating the spokes, bring the needle up near the center, between two spokes. Weave the needle under every other spoke (not going into the fabric).

3. Continue weaving the thread over and under alternate spokes. Weave part of the circle or the whole circle. Push previous lines of weaving snugly toward the center of the circle to create deeper dimension. Once you've finished weaving, pull the thread to the back of the fabric.

Spider Wheel

Also known as a whipped wheel or raised wheel, this technique is similar to the woven wheel but has a more dimensional surface texture. Instead of weaving, you'll whip the thread around each spoke, emphasizing the initial star shape.

1. Mark the outline of a circle on your fabric. Stitch an even number of evenly spaced spokes. With each spoke, bring the needle up at the edge of the outline and take it down directly opposite.

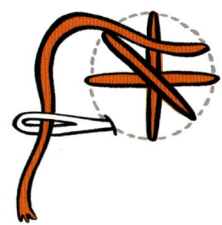

2. After creating the spokes, bring the needle up near the center, between two spokes. Pulling the thread counterclockwise over the first spoke, slip the needle under both the first spoke and the second spoke (not going into the fabric).

3. Pull the needle and thread through. Wrap the thread over the second spoke and then under both the second and third spokes. (You go over a single spoke and under two spokes for each stitch.)

4. Weave just a few rounds, leaving some of the spokes exposed, or fill in the entire circle. Once you've finished weaving, pull the thread to the back of the fabric.

Wrapped Stitch

By wrapping an existing stitch, such as the chain stitch or backstitch, this technique creates a rope-like effect. Choose either a thread that matches the color of the original line of stitching or a contrasting color to emphasize the diagonal stripes of the wrapped stitches. The needle goes into the fabric only at the beginning and end of the line.

1. Bring up a needle threaded with contrast color at the end of the chain stitch or backstitch. Insert the needle underneath the next chain stitch or backstitch (not going through the fabric). Pull until it gently wraps over the stitch.

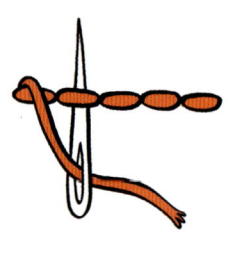

2. Repeat this wrapping motion over and under the existing stitches, always working in the same direction and never inserting the needle into the fabric.

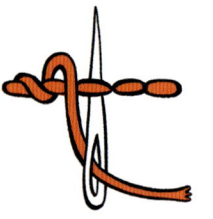

3. When finished, insert the needle back into the fabric on the right side and knot it at the back.

Blanket Stitch

The blanket stitch is used decoratively, for finishing edges, or to finish patches of fabric. Like the chain stitch (see page 181), each stitch is held down by the stitch that comes after it, so be sure to tuck your thread behind the needle each time before pulling through. This stitch looks like little stems coming off a straight line of stitches, but each stem is actually part of the straight line.

1. After bringing the needle out to begin, insert the tip about ¼ inch away from and ¼ inch above where the thread came out.

2. Bring the tip of the needle out on the same line where the last stitch came out (the needle should be perpendicular to the line), tucking the thread behind the tip of the needle before pulling through.

3. Continue, inserting the needle about ¼ inch away from and ¼ inch above where the thread came out. If it helps, imagine this stitch as a series of squares in a row.

4. The needle should be inserted at a right angle to the direction of the line of stitching, catching the thread behind the needle for each stitch.

5. To finish, secure the final stitch with a tiny tack by inserting the needle on the other side of the loop.

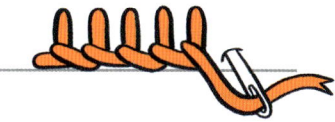

Curved Blanket Stitch

This uses the same technique as the blanket stitch (facing page) but on a curved line or in a circle. You may stitch with the spokes fanning outward or heading inward. It helps to draw both arc shapes, the inner and the outer edge of the flower or wheel, before stitching. Both of the motifs below work best if the stitches are fairly close together, no more than ¼ inch apart.

Flower Motif

1. Begin with the thread coming out of the inner circle. Insert the needle into the outer edge of the circle and bring it out at the inner edge a tiny bit away from where the thread came out. Tuck the thread behind the tip of the needle before pulling through.

2. Repeat with wider spacing between stitches on the outer curved line, and barely any spacing on the inner curved line.

3. Continue on around the curved lines. End with a tiny tack to secure the last stitch, which should connect the last stitch to the beginning of the first stitch.

Wheel Motif

1. Begin with the thread coming out of the outer edge. Insert the needle into the inner edge.

2. Aim the point back through the outer edge and tuck the thread behind the needle before pulling through.

3. Repeat, stitching close to the first stitch on the inner circle, with wider spacing between stitches on the outer circle.

4. Continue the stitch. You create an arcing loop by inserting the needle very close to the previous stitch on the inner edge.

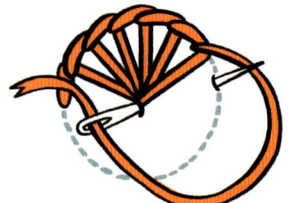

Overlapped Blanket Stitch

The blanket stitch can fill areas with a very open, gridlike effect if you overlap rows. This technique looks best when contained within a solid outline, such as the backstitch or chain stitch.

1. Make a row of blanket stitches at the bottom of the area to be filled, with the spokes of each stitch reaching the edge of this area.

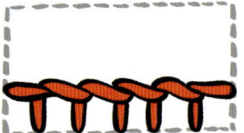

2. On the next row, overlap each spoke of the backstitch on the main line of the previous row. To create staggered squares, each spoke should be in between the spokes of the previous row.

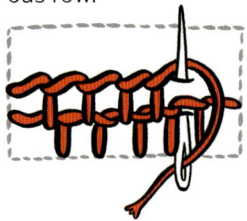

3. When you've reached the opposite edge of the area to be filled, use straight stitches to complete the grid, overlapping the last line of blanket stitch.

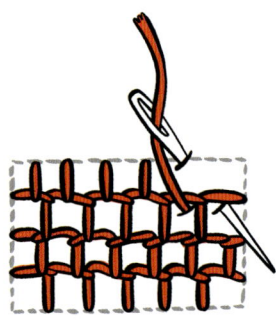

Alter the number of stitches in each line to fill shapes other than rectangles.

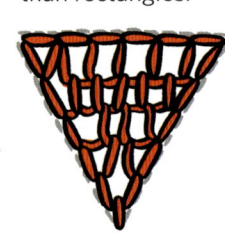

Chain Stitch

For the chain stitch, you'll insert the needle back into the same spot the thread came out of. If you do not catch the thread behind the needle on each stitch, it will not create the stitch and you are left with a loose loop that quickly unravels. For tips on creating points and turning corners with the chain stitch, see page 182.

1. Bring the needle out at the end of the stitch line, then insert the needle into the fabric at this same point, but don't pull through yet!

2. Position the tip of the needle to come out ¼ inch away from where it went in.

TUCK BEHIND NEEDLE

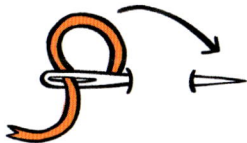

3. At this point, when you've got the needle coming out of the fabric, before you pull it through, tuck the thread behind the needle so that the next stitch catches this stitch.

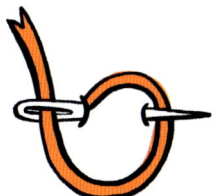

4. Pull the needle through until the loop is gently secured against where the thread comes out, but not so tight that the loop pulls on the loose thread. Now insert the needle back inside this loop, right where the thread just came out.

5. Bring the tip of the needle out ¼ inch down the stitch line, but don't pull through yet.

6. Tuck the thread behind the needle, then pull through until the stitch creates a gentle loop nestled into the previous loop.

7. To end the chain stitch, insert the needle into the fabric on the outside of this loop to tack down this last stitch and prevent all the stitches from coming undone. Either use a tiny stitch to create a blunt end or a long stitch for a tapered end.

PULL TO BACK

TO END

POINTS AND TURNS WITH CHAIN STITCH

When turning corners with a chain stitch, it's best to end the stitch and begin a new chain stitch at the corner, slightly overlapping the end stitch so there is no gap in the line where the new stitch begins (A).

To create tapered points with a chain stitch, stagger the threads at the beginning of the stitch so the loop is a little narrower (B).

Then continue normally. To end the stitch with a taper, create an elongated end stitch ¼ to ½ inch depending on how tapered you want the end (C). On sharp corners where two lines meet, slightly stagger the ends so that one line is shorter to create a more gentle tapered effect (D).

A. Turning corners

B. Beginning stitch with tapered end

C. Finishing stitch with tapered end

D. Staggered ends to create tapered point

Detached Chain Stitch

Often called the daisy stitch, a detached chain stitch is created with the first and last step of the chain stitch, securing the end of a single loop. Stitching in a circle makes sweet flowers.

1. Like with the chain stitch, bring the needle out at the end of the stitch line, then insert the needle into the fabric at this same point.

2. Position the tip of the needle to come out ¼ inch away from where it went in, and before you pull through, tuck the thread behind the needle.

3. Pull the needle through until the loop lies snug against the thread coming out of the middle, then tack down this stitch by inserting the needle into the outside of the loop.

Fly Stitch

The fly stitch creates little arrows that suggest a variety of forms. With the corner pointing up, they might be tiny trees or mountains. With the corner pointing down, they become birds on a horizon.

1. Instead of inserting the needle in the same spot the thread came out (like the chain stitch), you'll insert the needle about ¼ inch to the side of where the thread came out.

2. Bring the tip of the needle out about ¼ inch above and in the middle between these two points.

3. Before pulling the needle through, tuck the thread behind it.

4. Tack this stitch down by inserting the needle above this point (on the other side of the V shape made by the thread), creating a small stitch. Pull through to the back to secure.

Fly Stitch Variation

Use the fly stitch in multiples to create an arrow pattern by elongating the end stitch.

1. Follow steps 1 through 3 of the fly stitch instructions. Instead of tacking down this shape with a small stitch, insert the needle ¼ inch above the fly stitch and bring the tip of the needle out to the side at one end of the next fly stitch.

2. Insert the needle into the fabric on the other side. Bring it out at the end of the last tacked stitch and tuck the thread behind the needle tip before pulling through.

3. Continue to tack down the previous fly stitch with long stitches of equal length.

Double Chain Stitch

This stitch is great for finishing the edges of a design. Try accenting with French knots (see page 173) in the open spaces within the stitches or stitching multiple rows of double chain next to each other. The effect works best at stitch lengths of ¼ to ½ inch. Directions below are for a ¼-inch chain.

1. Bring the needle up at point A, then insert it at point B, bringing it out ¼ inch down.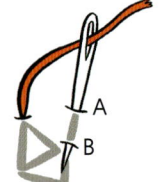

2. Tuck the thread behind the needle and pull it through.

3. Bring the needle up at point A again and bring it out ¼ inch down.

4. Tuck the thread behind the needle and pull through.

5. Continue, inserting each new stitch into the same spot as the previous anchor, inside the tuck.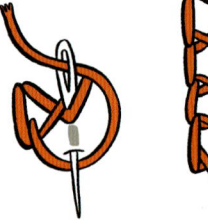

Magic Chain Stitch

By stitching with two different colors of threads at the same time, your chain stitch will alternate colors, creating a checkered effect. The technique takes a little extra handling, but the results are a delight! You should be very familiar with the chain stitch before attempting the magic chain stitch.

1. Thread the needle with two different colors of thread.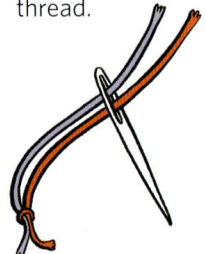

2. Just like the chain stitch, bring the needle out at the end of the stitch line, then insert the needle into the fabric at this same point, but don't pull through yet.

3. Position the tip of the needle to come out ¼ inch away from where it went in.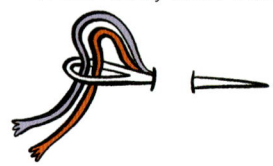

4. At this point, when you've got the needle coming out of the fabric, before you pull it through, tuck only *one color* of the thread behind the needle so that the next stitch catches this stitch.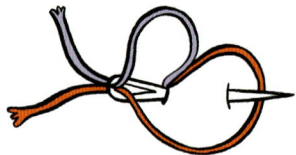

5. Pull the needle through until the loop is gently secured against where the thread comes out, allowing the untucked color to pull through at the beginning of the stitch. (You may need to tug the unused color so that only one color shows up on the front.) Now insert the needle back inside this loop, right where the thread just came out.

6. Bring the tip of the needle out ¼ inch down the stitch line, but don't pull through yet.

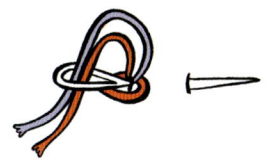

7. Tuck the *other color* thread behind the needle, then pull through until the stitch creates a gentle loop nestled into the previous loop. Pull the unused color to the back to hide it.

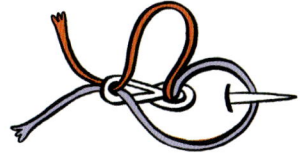

8. Alternate between colors for each stitch, tucking one color and then the other, pulling at whichever color wasn't used to get it to lie flat. To end the magic chain stitch, insert the needle into the fabric on the outside of this loop to tack down the last stitch using both colors of thread.

Feather Stitch

This simple stitch is bursting with potential. Once you've mastered the basic method, try switching it up a bit. Lengthen different parts of the legs, change the angle of each stitch, or make it closer together or farther apart.

1. After bringing the thread out at the top of the design, insert the needle about ¼ inch to the right of where the thread came out, similar to the fly stitch (see page 183).

2. Bring the tip of the needle out about ¼ inch below and in the middle between these two points, and tuck the thread behind the tip of the needle before pulling through.

3. Insert the needle about ¼ inch to the right of where the thread came out.

4. Bring the tip out about ¼ inch below and in the middle between these two points, tucking the thread behind the needle before pulling through.

5. Insert the needle ¼ inch to the left of where the thread came out, bringing the tip of the needle out ¼ inch below and to the middle, and tucking the thread before pulling through. Repeat from left to right. For a wide feather stitch, make three stitches to the right, then three stitches to the left.

ACKNOWLEDGMENTS

I'd like to extend my warmest, brightest thank-yous to all of my students, who continually inspire me and help me gain a deeper understanding of the materials and teachings through our time together; to my love, Nicholas, for your unending support and always encouraging me to make my work the best it could be; to my sweet baby girl for bringing so much light (often delaying deadlines in the process); to Jessica Adamson, without your help and talents much of this book wouldn't exist; to Hesh, for your energy and enthusiasm, and your wonderful team, Eliza and Dallas; to my mother and sister for being my core creative community; to Stacy Wakefield for guiding me on this path; to Alethea Morrison for your vision, support, collaboration, and patience; and to the rest of the team at Storey whose hands have touched this book, for your passion and hard work!

WITH GRATITUDE TO OUR PROFILED ARTISTS

Sarah K. Benning
@sarahkbenning
www.sarahkbenning.com

Valeria Duque
@vduquep

Beth Hoyes
@rabbithatdesigns

Anna Hultin
www.olandercoembroidery.com
@olandercoembroidery

Ciara LeRoy
www.prettystrangedesign.com
@prettystrangedesign

Lindzeanne
@lindzeanne

Gabriela Martínez Ortiz
www.gamaor.com
@gamaor

Elizabeth Pawle
www.elizabethpawle.com

Tessa Perlow
@tessa_perlow

Rebecca Ringquist
www.dropclothsamplers.com
@dropcloth

INDEX

Page numbers in *italics* indicate illustrations or photos.